Grace
in the
Grind

52 DEVOTIONS FOR
THRIVING IN THE WORKPLACE

WANDA MARIE THIBODEAUX

FOTC
FAITHFUL ON THE CLOCK
Minnesota | USA
faithfulontheclock.captivate.fm | faithfulontheclock.com

Grace in the Grind: 52 Devotions for Thriving in the Workplace

Christian Nonfiction

Copyright © 2025 Wanda Thibodeaux

Published by Faithful on the Clock
faithfulontheclock.captivate.fm | faithfulontheclock.com

Printed in the United States of America
First Edition

Paperback · ISBN: 978-1-968754-00-6
Hardcover · ISBN: 978-1-968754-01-3
Ebook · ISBN: 978-1-968754-02-0
Audiobook · ISBN: 978-1-968754-03-7

Cover design by Julie Karen Hodgins
juliekaren.com

For more information about the author or upcoming books, visit:
takingdictation.com
wandathibodeaux.com

For every professional seeking joy, clarity, courage, and deeper relationship with God—thank you for choosing grace and believing, even while facing weariness and struggling through the middle of the grind, that faith and work do belong together.

How to Use This Devotional

In August 2021, I started the *Faithful on the Clock* podcast under a simple premise: Stressful psychological dissonance occurs when the values of our workplace don't align with the values of our faith. Resolving this mental clash enables us to be who God created us to be, feel comfortable, and find success.

This devotional brings scriptural concepts into how you interact with colleagues, approach competition, develop policy, lead, and pursue career advancement. It offers challenges to stretch you, bring your reflection into practice, and grow your faith. Professionals are great action-takers. So, this is not a read-it-and-be-done kind of devotional. You're meant to get up and go do! Take notes as you complete the challenges to help you process the journey.

This book is not dated or arranged by season or theme because the integration of faith and work rarely unfolds in neat categories. Feel free to read these devotions in order, skip around based on what you're feeling, or return to them as new challenges arise.

At the end of every devotion are four reflection questions that complement the Scripture verse for the week. You're welcome to use your own notebook, a cloud-based word processing app, or even a video diary to answer the questions. Answering a reflection question every day or two is a good way to ensure you don't rush through your answers. But you might consider all the questions throughout the entire week and then document everything you've contemplated. Work in whatever way gets you into a natural, consistent rhythm.

As you work your way through the devotions, make full use of the endnotes. These provide sources for assertions made in the devotions, but also extended materials, such as episodes of the *Faithful on the Clock* podcast, YouTube videos, and long-form social media posts. These are included both to lend credibility and to add value by expanding the insights available on the topics.

You also will find an Additional Resources page at the end of this book. This page lists Christian organizations that can further support your professional and faith development.

In the ebook edition of this text, listings on the Additional Resources page are hyperlinked, while endnotes are underlined and hyperlinked. For print and audiobook editions, you can visit faithfulontheclock.com/graceinthegrind/endnotes and faithfulontheclock.com/graceinthegrind/additionalresources to access hyperlinked versions.

Part of the value of using devotionals is the intimate personal time they help create to spend with God. But as Christians, we're not meant to lean only on ourselves. Rather, we are to encourage and lift one another up (1 Thessalonians 5:11; Ecclesiastes 4:12; Galatians 6:1-10). Additionally, leaders encourage team cohesion for both productivity and morale. Reading this devotional with a few colleagues might clarify collective values, strengthen interpersonal bonds, and keep God at the helm of your business. You can use the reflection questions to facilitate group study and open communication.

This devotional uses the New International Version (NIV) translation of the Bible. But using different translations can help believers be more satisfied in the full depth and wisdom of Scripture. Looking at verses from many angles also paradoxically can ensure that personal interpretative biases don't hijack the big-picture meaning of the Word, which improves the likelihood of proper real-life application. For these reasons, I encourage you to read each verse in a variety of translations.

My prayer as you begin this devotional journey is that it will become easier for you over time to reflect Who God is and to advocate for Him in the way you work. May each devotion encourage and inspire you to find the deeper connection and joy He wants for you.

Contents

Week 1
Prepare with Rest

Six days you shall labor and do all your work, but the seventh day is a sabbath to the Lord your God. On it you shall not do any work, neither you, nor your son or daughter, nor your male or female servant, nor your ox, your donkey or any of your animals, nor any foreigner residing in your towns, so that your male and female servants may rest, as you do.—Deuteronomy 5:13-14

Have you ever struggled to slow down?

The pressure to perform and compete can tempt us to push time with God to the back burner in the name of *being prepared*.

But science now tells us that, to do our best, the brain and body need time to repair.[1] The spirit needs time to absorb and learn.

In Genesis 1 and 2:1-3, we learn that God took time throughout the creation process to recognize and reflect on the goodness of what He was doing. When His work was finished, He could have gone directly to the next thing—God doesn't require rest in the same way we do. The fact He *didn't* immediately proceed to something else even when there was no physical need to wait shows that the decision to rest was also about the value of being mindful.

When God commanded us to make the seventh day a Sabbath, He wanted to ensure that we could take the rest we *do* need. But He also wanted us to take the lesson of mindfulness He had modeled and to reflect on the goodness of what He did, is doing, and will do. It's time set aside to help us remember Who He is.

In a particularly rough period of my life, my 90-hour work weeks felt necessary—keeping my nose to the grindstone kept us financially afloat while giving me a distraction from feeling helpless, unappreciated, and vocationally stuck. I told myself I could handle it, but I'd joke with my husband—only halfway—about running away to live in the forest with the gnomes. The exhausted part of me wanted out.

I was functioning. *But I wasn't living.*

God isn't satisfied to have us simply existing like this. His vision is for us to be fully connected to each other and to Him (John 3:16, 13:34-35; 1 Corinthians 12).

The Sabbath offers a combination of physical recuperation and mental surety of God. In this way, *the Sabbath isn't just recovery. It's simultaneously also the strengthening of our bond with Him and good preparation for what is yet to come.*

Tim Doremus, campus pastor for Life Church, shares a quirk someone showed him about the creation story. The sequential order given in the Scriptures is not morning to evening, but evening to morning.[2] Doremus asserts that this reversal is the alternative rhythm we are meant to have but seldom live. Instead of starting with our tasks and treating rest like a reward, we're meant to rest first and treat the repose like fueling up, so we can deliver everything God has called us to give.

That's worth clinging to the next time we're tempted to give up our weekend or evening to put in more hours.

Challenge

Pick 5 minutes out of the day to spend time with God. Gradually increase the time in whatever increment is doable for you. The goal isn't to abandon your tasks, but rather to learn to allow yourself to be fully present and rest with Him.

To gain the efficiency and accountability you need for this, use time management or automation tools and communicate transparently with friends and family. Be honest with yourself about when you can delegate, postpone a task, or avoid micromanaging.

Reflection Questions

1. What is your favorite way to recuperate when you need a break from work?

2. What usually keeps you from preparing on the Sabbath (or in the evenings) by resting and reflecting? What would it take to remove those obstacles?

3. How do gig or remote work options impact your ability to keep the Sabbath? How might they affect our ability as a culture to observe regular rest?

4. How might you address conflicts that arise from your decision to keep the Sabbath holy?

Week 2
Flourish by Blessing

But blessed is the one who trusts in the Lord, whose confidence is in him. They will be like a tree planted by the water that sends out its roots by the stream. It does not fear when heat comes; its leaves are always green. It has no worries in a year of drought and never fails to bear fruit. —Jeremiah 17:7-8

Millennia after Jeremiah 17:7-8 was written, the image of a flourishing plant has become nearly synonymous with professional growth. We're supposed to constantly develop.

The issue is that, instead of trusting God to get the growth we desire, we trust our own skills, knowledge, and merit to "do the deep work," find our own epiphanies, and mitigate risk. When we manage to develop a new branch, we want to crow about the effort we put in to be better.

Our attitude toward wealth acquisition isn't any better. We readily take credit for every cent we have and fiercely assert we've earned each one (see Week 41).

But we're all human. Consequently, there's no way we can plan or mitigate perfectly. We have far less control than we believe we do. What we work for can be turned into dust in mere seconds.

Trusting in ourselves thus bears no meaning. We can flourish only by the blessing of God, Who knows the care each of us needs to reach our full potential.

If we see God as a Master Gardener for our lives, we must also recognize that there might be moments when storms painfully break us. We can know in those moments that God has the power to restore the branches that were lost, to heal us back to where we were—to what feels *normal*.

But what if the healing and restoration don't come? Should we simply assume we are forgotten or that we've somehow lost His blessing?

In Season 3, Episode 2 of *The Chosen*, James the Lesser (Little James) asks Jesus why He has not physically healed him. Jesus' answer, as portrayed in the show, is that God has entrusted Little James with a different kind of testimony: Instead of telling a "typical" story of healing, Little James can show what persisting in faith *without* healing looks like.[3]

Like the storm-beaten tree bears new shoots even as its gnarly burls remain, showing all the tree has endured, we can continue to grow in the light of God despite suffering or scars. We might not get what we expected or asked for, but we can be blessed instead with the deeper gift of *despite everything* faith (see Week 34).

Real respect and love of God trusts His discernment in blessing, refusal, or even retraction. As Job aptly reflected, "The Lord gave and the Lord has taken away; may the name of the Lord be praised" (Job 1:21).

Challenge

Plant some seeds in a container you can keep in a bright spot in your home or office. Water the seeds as needed for the plant variety and conditions in your space. Each time you tend to the plant, reflect on how you can flourish when you invite the Father, Son, and Holy Spirit to guide and nurture your life.

Reflection Questions

1. Think about a time when you had trouble trusting in God for your growth. What was behind the lack of trust?

2. What are you tempted to put your trust in when your faith falters?

3. Have you ever been frustrated by your pace or style of growth compared to others? How might verses such as 2 Peter 3:8-9; Proverbs 16:9; and Ecclesiastes 3:11 offer encouragement?

4. What can you do to model God and be trustworthy to others?

Week 3
Trust God to Safeguard

Do not store up for yourselves treasures on earth, where moths and vermin destroy, and where thieves break in and steal. But store up for yourselves treasures in heaven, where moths and vermin do not destroy, and where thieves do not break in and steal. For where your treasure is, there your heart will be also.—Matthew 6:19-21

Professionals are experts at "biggering." We strive endlessly to get more clients, customers, money, offices, products, and stores.

Many of us also associate materialism with success. We buy nice homes, clothes, or other items to prove to ourselves and others that we've "made it."

When I was a teenager, I bought my first car—a used Pontiac Grand Am—for $1,300. It looked awful. But it proved to be a workhorse, getting me through high school *and* my undergraduate degrees. My husband and I hauled it behind our moving van to Minnesota, where it transported my husband to and from work.

Replacing the car eventually became a safety necessity. My husband took classically cliché pictures of me sitting on the hoods of the new vehicles we bought, as we were proud we could afford them. It was only years later that I looked back at the Grand Am and appreciated the value of the freedom it had made possible.[4]

This "biggering" trend isn't merely egotism. It reflects our innate, deeper need to be seen and have influence. It also shows a subconscious fear—driven by many broken systems, traumas, and the cultural ideology of independence—that socially driven security is fickle.

In this context, it's understandable that people would seek to safeguard themselves. It's not something to shame anybody for.

But when we seek to safeguard ourselves, we don't allow God to safeguard us.

Nothing is supposed to supersede God. If we constantly are thinking about how to increase what we have or get what we need, self-safeguarding can become an idol we prioritize over Him.

If we can resist the temptation to be our own protector and provider, God can meet the immediate needs we have and give us access to the long-term rewards of Heaven. When we treat Him as our treasure, we keep perspective about what matters.

All this dramatically can shift our gratitude experience.[5] Gratitude is directly proportional to the value we place on something. If we learn to place value on the right things, it is easy to be grateful for them. When God has the highest value in our lives, expressing gratitude *for Him as He is*—not just the blessings He might grant us—no longer is challenging.

Trusting God for provision and being grateful doesn't mean sitting in passivity. There's maturity in accepting some responsibility and accountability, and showing up to take appropriate action is part of healthy relational reciprocity. That's why, even when God offered manna in the desert, He still expected the people of Israel to go out and gather it up (Exodus 13).

Give Him control, but then do the part He trusts you with.

Challenge

Find at least one thing you can get rid of in your house or apartment. Don't choose something you were going to get rid of anyway. Instead, get rid of something you put some value on. Repeat the process regularly until your willingness to give reflects your trust that God will always provide.

Letting go doesn't mean wastefulness—it can mean redirecting value to where it's most needed. Suppose you have a stuffed animal from when you were a kid. It might have a lot of sentimental value. But it might do more good and bring more joy if you donated it to a children's hospital.

Alternatively, set a cap on what you will obtain and keep, such as donating to charity if your income exceeds a certain amount per year.

Any charity can be a good target. But people often need only a small amount of help to prevent their circumstances from snowballing into disaster.[6] Consider giving to organizations that attempt to stop this downward spiral, such as an automotive shop that does free service to ensure people can continue to get to work.

Reflection Questions

1. What do you think "treasures in Heaven" includes?

2. How does Matthew 6:19-21 connect to the idea of the inheritance granted to us through Jesus?

3. What kind of things are you tempted to store up the most? What do those things represent to you?

4. What do you include in your bare minimum to be happy? Why? How might God redefine that minimum for you?

Week 4

Use What's Positive to Stay Balanced

Finally, brothers and sisters, whatever is true, whatever is noble, whatever is right, whatever is pure, whatever is lovely, whatever is admirable—if anything is excellent or praiseworthy—think about such things.—Philippians 4:8

In contemporary business culture, there's a massive emphasis on positivity. The idea is that how we think and feel influences the results we achieve. A good attitude can reduce the stress that can lead to poor judgment, an overly critical self-interpretation of skills, or apathy. It literally wires the brain to overcome negativity bias and be more likely to spot and apply what's beautiful, optimistic, and hopeful.[7]

But there's a risk of using Philippians 4:8 to create *toxic* positivity and brush all negative elements in our lives under the rug. We might even spiritually bypass everything that's difficult and tell ourselves God will do all the heavy lifting for us.

Philippians 4:8 is not about hiding hurt, hardship, and fatigue behind cat posters.[8] I've felt the sting of being ghosted by clients when I needed to be paid. I've left Zoom calls trying to reassure myself that the problems my employer was encountering were fixable, only to have the uneasiness in my gut affirm the business would die (it did). Like George Bailey in *It's a Wonderful Life*, I've had to make impossible choices between pursuing calling and protecting the wellbeing of people I deeply love.[9,10] Those experiences have played a part in shaping me and will be part of my spirit forever. To be authentic, I have to acknowledge that.

Rather, Philippians 4:8 is about recognizing life is not *only* hardship. When we consider everything that contrasts our struggles, we can maintain the healthy perspective necessary to avoid sinking into anxiety, depression, and other mental health problems.

Focusing on good things also gives us a reminder of God's creative, merciful nature and authority. No matter how bleak things might seem or how powerless we might feel, nothing can disrupt Him. Reflecting on all the beauty and marvels of the world, we can sit in perfect confidence, knowing He can overcome and that goodness exists, even in the middle of pain.

Challenge

Whenever you see something good or marvelous happen throughout the day, make a note of it. Acknowledge how the good stuff adds up over time to anchor you in God's grace, even if you're surrounded by what's tough.

In the evening, prepare for the next day by 1) using a gratitude journal to reflect on the good, 2) using your reflections to build next steps and decisions, and 3) giving God thanks (see Weeks 1 and 3).

Reflection Questions

1. Considering Philippians 4:8, what do you think is true, noble, right, pure, lovely, admirable, excellent, or praiseworthy?

2. When you think about these types of things, how do you feel? When you don't?

3. How might a recognition of God's goodness and steady authority as a loving Father change your relationship to Him? To others? To yourself?

4. What habits could you develop to see more positive things in the world, even as you admit and address what's negative?

Week 5
Find Freedom in Smart Rules

*I will walk about in freedom, for I have sought out your
precepts.—Psalm 119:45*

Often, professionals see precepts—rules or guidelines—in terms
of risk management. Subsequently, we focus on what we're
prohibited from doing.

But good guidelines keep us from getting into trouble. With better
focus, protection, and clarity about what should be done, we can
more easily unify, creatively collaborate, and proceed without
conflict. Rules thus are central to honing and reaching our vision.

In the same way, God's rules aren't meant to restrict us from
success or enjoyment. Rather, they're designed to provide guardrails
so we know exactly what to do in whatever circumstances we
encounter.

When we seek out the precepts He gave, we can also stay away
from people or darker forces that would control us, because we have
no confusion about Who has power and what to prioritize.

This ability to stay focused can support good decisions and let us
live with a clear conscience, free from guilt that might come from
hurting ourselves, others, or God.

If you find yourself feeling confused or overwhelmed, turn to
God's Word to set some foundational boundaries. Then consider
what other positive boundaries might serve the unique demands of
your life and work.

Challenge

Identify one area of your life where you've experienced pain, confusion, or unpredictability. Maybe that's the threat of a divorce, lack of clarity about how to deal with a business partner, or taking care of your body.

Look up what the Bible has to say on that topic, paying attention to God's balance of lawgiving and grace. Make a step-by-step action plan for how you might implement those wise guidelines in your everyday life. Acknowledge potential pitfalls or temptations you might encounter as you try to build those new guardrails.

Reflection Questions

1. In what ways have you sought to know—or sidestep—what God does and does not want you to do?

2. What helped you overcome times in your life when you felt restricted?

3. How do you define freedom from an Earthly perspective? Spiritual?

4. How might having an attitude of freedom through God influence your interactions and professional or spiritual success?

Week 6
Forgive for Joy and Purposeful Pursuit

But with you there is forgiveness, so that we can, with reverence,
serve you. —Psalm 130:4

More than likely, we'll all experience hurt at work—the coworker who takes credit for our work, the boss who yells at us, the board that forces a complete restructuring that costs us our job, or teammates who don't respond or reciprocate.

The first instinct we might have when we face these situations is to put the people involved on our you-know-what list. The temptation can be high to trumpet our wound under the pretense of warning others about the offender.

Or, we might turn everything toward ourselves and get lost in guilt and shame: *If I were such a great person and professional, why didn't they treat me better?*

One experience with a ghostwriting company was particularly painful for me: I served for years as the go-to wordsmith editors trusted to meet rush deadlines and revise pieces from others that weren't working. Eventually, however, despite reassurances there would be plenty of work, the company started to struggle. I had no choice but to move on after hearing on social media—not in a meeting—that the company was done. There was no parting acknowledgement, and I didn't hear back on my requests for a letter of recommendation. *After working with clear loyalty and expertise, why wasn't I worth more than gaslighting and silence?*

In either case, the feelings of sadness, frustration, or offense aren't going to move us forward. They only leave us stuck in the past and questioning the value of our own authenticity. They make it hard for any of us to have joy in the moment and consider our potential and future. What's more, there are very real ramifications for having unresolved feuds in the office, one being that others become leery to trust and do business with us.

20

If we can't connect because of unresolved conflicts, it's emotionally and logistically more difficult to follow through on the work God has called us to do. Let's aim to forgive—and, if possible, reconcile—so we're free to pursue whatever God assigns to us.

Challenge

Write a letter to someone to ask for, grant, or say thank you for forgiveness. You don't have to send this letter, but do so if you can.

Write a second letter to yourself expressing self-forgiveness for something work-related that has caused you guilt or shame. If you feel comfortable, share this letter with a trusted friend, work mentor, pastor, or counselor to open a conversation about your growth.

Reflection Questions

1. Why do you think God forgives us?

2. What has made it difficult or easy for you to forgive yourself or others in the past? In your current situation?

3. How can you show God, others, and yourself that you are grateful for the forgiveness you receive?

4. How do you practice both forgiveness and accountability— in your personal life and in your company's expectations or policies?

Week 7
Ask for Wisdom

So I turned my mind to understand, to investigate and to search
out wisdom and the scheme of things and to understand the
stupidity of wickedness and the madness of folly.
—Ecclesiastes 7:25

As King David reached the end of his reign, he had a lot to be proud of. The tribes of Israel finally were unified. He'd subdued many of the enemies that might have been a threat.

Yet, the tendency Israel had to stray from God and find fault with its leadership had been a persistent problem ever since Moses first led the people from Egypt. The threat of losing the newfound peace and morality King David had forged was real.

When King Solomon inherited the kingdom, he understood he could not protect or expand Israel's newly unified empire unless he could figure out what was good and what was evil. So, when God told King Solomon in a dream to ask for anything, King Solomon asked for wisdom (1 Kings 3:5-15).

Today, foolishness is alive and well, including in the corporate space. Scandals, misinformation, disinformation, and poor analysis abound. It can be confusing to know where truth ends and malicious guile begins.

Now more than ever, discernment separates a poor leader from an outstanding one. Like King Solomon, we need to ask God to give us the capacity to understand and interpret knowledge well.

But King Solomon's story is as much about humility as it is wisdom (see Week 22). Showing love for his people, he put them first and asked God for the wisdom necessary to ensure Israel's success. Because King Solomon's heart was in the right place, God gave him not just the wisdom he'd asked for, but also all the wealth and honor he had been willing to sacrifice.

When we face more than we can handle alone or don't know how to do the job in front of us, it's tempting to "save face" by pretending we understand. But because giving in to that temptation—be it from fear, pride, or other reasons—means we never are truly authentic about who we are or what we need, our performative strength ultimately leaves us isolated and starving for rest.

Like King Solomon, we can admit our weaknesses, ask God to give us what we need to faithfully serve well, and then surround ourselves with wise people who can keep us aligned with His direction. In that prudence, we can always find safety.

Challenge

If you don't already have any, find good mentors you can go to when you are lost or confused. Remember here that the best mentors often are not the famous gurus who are booked for the next decade. They're the neighbors, pastors, and other leaders within your own community who can understand and empathize with the circumstances you're in.

Even though mentors are essential, wisdom also comes through study. Reading widely helps you think more clearly and act with good judgment.

Set a foundation by reading the Word regularly. Then select material from outside your industry, as information from one discipline often has applications in another. Look at the writings of philosophers who were the thought leaders of their cultures and times, as they can provide a range of concepts that broaden your thinking.

Keep in mind through these activities that perfect agreement isn't the point—sometimes the greatest surety we get comes from needing to defend our ideas and rationales against echo chambers. The goal is to expose yourself to different viewpoints to learn and clarify your own values.

Reflection Questions

1. What is something you feel technically or philosophically confused about?

2. How do you usually decide what's true or good? Are those methods working well? Why or why not?

3. What is one piece of wisdom you could share with someone else?

4. Who might help you gain more wisdom in your job or personal life?

Week 8
Praise with Full, Messy Feelings

But I will sing of your strength, in the morning I will sing of your love; for you are my fortress, my refuge in times of trouble.
—*Psalm 59:16*

Have you ever had a day—or even a few minutes—where you were just so light and joyful that you found yourself humming, dancing, or giving an excited squeal?

That kind of delight—that feeling of overflowing joy—is what being connected to God can bring. When we're aware of what He's done and Who He is, sometimes we just can't keep it in.

Praise is allowed to happen whenever the Spirit moves us. But in Psalm 59:16, the emphasis is on praising God in the morning. Productivity and success gurus often emphasize that the way we start our morning sets the tone for the entire day. By choosing to begin the day by lifting our voice in gratitude and enthusiasm, we prime our mind, body, and being to operate in rhythm with Him.

Singing to God doesn't require any formal music training. It's OK if we don't sound like popular artists on the radio or online. It's not about being on key (although that's nice). It's about music having the power to release the genuine, messy, indescribable emotions we have when we consider how wonderful it is that the God Who built the universe with His voice is the same God Who sacrificed everything and cherishes every hair on our head.

Many poetic Scripture verses convey the idea of mountains, stars, water, and everything on the Earth praising God (e.g., Psalm 148). We often take these metaphorically.

But the Pythagorean concept of the music of the spheres still has weight, with scientists learning that space and the world are not as quiet as people might think: Plasma waves that can be converted to sound are present between Saturn and its moon (Enceladus).[11] Plants can emit sound.[12] "Live," sonorous rocks, when struck, can ring like bells.[13]

You might have blown a dog whistle, heard nothing, yet watched a dog rub or cover its ears. *Just because something isn't immediately perceptible to us doesn't mean it's not happening.* Perhaps the world is already praising God and we merely need to join in.

Challenge

Make playlists of some of your favorite music. The tracks don't necessarily have to be contemporary Christian worship music. Simply choose pieces that help you connect to God in a deep way. Some of my personal favorites include *In the Bleak Midwinter* (Harold Darke), *The Ludlows* (James Horner), and *Joy* (for King + Country).

If you feel it might be helpful, explore the ISO principle from music therapy.[14] This principle asserts that you should start with music that matches your current mood and then gradually shift to music that supports the emotional, spiritual, or nervous system state you want to cultivate. For instance, you could create a playlist for the morning that guides you from a calm, meditative state to an energetic one. Consider including meditation tracks such as *Earth Om* (Byron Metcalf), which are specifically designed to support regulation utilizing the science around auditory and parasympathetic processing.

Some tracks can stick with you and have meaning for life. But you might find that your playlists have to change to accommodate how you've grown or what you've been thrown into—after my mother passed away, the theme to *To Kill a Mockingbird* (Elmer Bernstein) was too wounding for me. Adjust your playlists however you need to, but let them be an altar where your emotional honesty and God's presence can meet.

Reflection Questions

1. If you're not particularly musical and are a little shy about using your voice to praise God, what other ways might you "sing?"

2. Most of us find it easy to sing when we feel good. Why is it important to continue to sing even when you feel spiritually or emotionally low ("bleh") (Job 1:21)?

3. What happens when others see you singing the praises of God?

4. How do songs of praise compare to the secular songs you enjoy?

Week 9
Let Evidence of God Affirm Faith

For since the creation of the world God's invisible qualities—his eternal power and divine nature—have been clearly seen, being understood from what has been made, so that people are without excuse.—Romans 1:20

When you were a kid, did you ever look under your bed to make sure there weren't any monsters?

What about checking your work bag (again) to make sure you've packed your tablet?

These activities are just two examples of the fact that seeing something helps the brain recognize and remember it as real. That's why businesses use photos and charts in reports and presentations, and why leaders encourage others to use vision boards to "manifest their dreams." If we can see it, it's not as hard to accept it.

We can see evidence of the abstract qualities of God throughout the world. In the same way a smile proves kindness, volcanoes or the strength of the alligator's jaws hold His power, the flow of a waterfall shares His gracefulness, and the orange blush of an autumn leaf confirms His joy. The entire world serves as a symphonic, sensory reminder of His existence and desire for us to grasp the paradoxical, complex simplicity of Who He is.

But God has used the fact that vision promotes psychological acceptance in the ministry of Jesus, too (e.g., John 9, 20).

Perhaps the clearest portrait of vision removing doubt is in the story of Thomas, who believed that Jesus had been resurrected once he saw the wounds on Jesus' body (John 20:24-29). Yet, in that encounter, Jesus says, "Because you have seen me, you have believed; blessed are those who have not seen and yet have believed."

Jesus was noting the wonderful faith it takes to believe in the Messiah and His mission without having seen Him. This point is critical, because it means that *even though visual cues certainly help grow faith, they're not a requirement for it.* Entrepreneurs, who often must champion concepts that can't yet be seen, can understand the value of this sentiment especially well.

Once we see evidence of God, that evidence has a way of shaping how we see ourselves, others, our circumstances, our work, and wherever we might be. As it did for the disciples, it can prompt us to abandon what we once wanted to pursue, so that we might better glorify God. As C.S. Lewis wrote in *Is Theology Poetry* in *The Weight of Glory and Other Essays*, "I believe in Christianity as I believe that the sun has risen, not only because I see it, but because by it I see everything else."

Challenge

Take some pictures of things in God's world you think are amazing. You can put your photos in a special album, faith journal, or scrapbook; share them with friends or on social media with a note about why you think they're incredible; or use them as your digital avatars. Let this practice train your eyes to see God's fingerprints in the world around you—not just with your camera, but with your heart.

Reflection Questions

1. What have you physically seen that has helped increase your faith? What did it teach you?

2. What specific qualities of God do you see in what's around you? What seems to testify to those qualities the most?

3. Aside from the photo challenge offered for this devotion, how can you share this evidence with other people?

4. What is your favorite story from the Bible—or from people you know—about how God has manifested His power and nature?

Week 10

Turn Enemies into Iron-Sharpens-Iron Allies

"You have heard that it was said, 'Love your neighbor and hate your enemy.' But I tell you, love your enemies and pray for those who persecute you, that you may be children of your Father in heaven."—Matthew 5:43-45

In the corporate space, we frame everything as a fierce, dog-eat-dog competition between enemies where businesses are willing to push the envelope of morality to win.

Even within our own company, we might not be safe. After all, who are our coworkers, except others who are seeking the same recognition and promotions we are? They could be secretly analyzing every possible method to outdo us.

At least, that's the worry.

The overall undercurrent is that it would be naïve and foolish to ignore how far others might go to secure their own success—trust is for the stupid.

Yet, Jesus challenges us to undo the enemy mindset.

By turning enemies into allies, we open the door to collaboration and innovation that wouldn't be possible if we worked alone.

But more importantly, in showing compassion, empathy, and love even to those who would harm us, we raise the possibility that others, seeing our behavior, might come to seek the God we follow. It reminds people that God never intended "us" versus "them," but rather a single flock (John 10:16). Because Earthly competition is meaningless in the context of eternity, it's better to see others as the brothers and sisters they are.

When disagreements occur or there can be only one #1 player, mutual respect and good sportsmanship can protect everyone involved and keep us from sinful behavior. An iron-sharpens-iron attitude will always attract more support and success than dog-eat-dog, as it's built on integrity rather than fear.

Challenge

Our instinct is often to protect our place or edge. But God invites us to practice generosity—even with those who seem like rivals—to build trust, diffuse fear, and open space for grace.

Find a competing business in your industry. Alternatively, identify a colleague whose skills, knowledge, or experience you sometimes feel threatened by. Find a simple way to show good, loving sportsmanship, such as letting them know about a new industry event or sending a note of congratulations.

Reflection Questions

1. Who do you consider to be a personal or professional enemy right now? Why?

2. How do you think your personal or professional life would change if the enemies you have were to become allies with you—or at least, were respectful?

3. What do you think your enemies need?

4. What can you do to reduce unnecessary conflict or build healthier relationships in the future—especially in competitive environments?

Week 11
Let Jesus Recover You

For the Son of Man came to seek and to save the lost.—Luke 19:10

A while back, I hunted on my laptop for a file I wanted to include in my online portfolio. Just when I was ready to pull out the last of my hair and give up, I found the file sitting happily in the portfolio folder I'd forgotten was right in plain sight on my main desktop. My subsequent face-palming was spectacular.

Maybe you're not quite at the age where you lose your reading glasses on top of your head. But you've probably hunted around for your car keys, used the "Find My Device" feature to locate your phone, or thrown up your hands during laundry at the loss of another sock.

No matter what the loss was, you probably didn't enjoy it all that much, and you probably tried to ensure it wouldn't happen again.

Professionals are all about risk mitigation and recovery. We want to lose as little as possible, and when we do lose, to recover as quickly as we can. That's because the ability to self-protect can mean we advance in our career or gain market share despite adversities that might get in our way (see Week 3).

But every one of us is lost in the sense that we are tied to the fall of Adam and Eve in the garden of Eden. Many of us know *of* God, but we don't wholeheartedly try to honor Him. Some of us openly deny Him and assert He doesn't exist at all.

In all cases, Jesus is our ultimate recovery tool. God knows that you are worth more than any S&P or Fortune 100 company, and He safeguarded your position with Him from day one.

Plotting out the steps necessary to ensure you could come to His Kingdom as a full heir was no simple feat—there can be dozens, hundreds, or even thousands of variables to consider when trying to assess the best protection and recovery route. Yet, God knew every miniscule move to take, right down to the person Mary could get swaddling clothes from as she went into labor.

During the recovery process, we often make a sacrifice, such as losing a little data. God's sacrifice to recover us was far deeper and more valuable: It cost Him His Son.

When we lose something or need to reposition, let's recall the recovery that really matters. God didn't perform it lightly, and we can live with the intention of making Him feel no regret about it.

Challenge

Go on a scavenger hunt by yourself or with your team. Alternatively, search your house for something you've been meaning to look for. After your search, talk or journal about the effort you went through and the emotions you had when you found (or couldn't find) what you were looking for.

Take time to reflect on the truth that, just as Jesus described with the parables of the lost sheep, lost coin, and the Prodigal Son, God seeks you with deep compassion (Luke 15). He likewise celebrates as soon as you are back in the safety of His green pastures (Psalm 23).

Reflection Questions

1. Have you ever lost something of value (e.g., a wallet, phone, etc.)? What did you do when you found it was missing?

2. In what areas can you admit that you might be currently—but temporarily—lost to God?

3. How long do you think God would search for you? Why? What does the Bible say about it (e.g., Hosea; Psalm 139)?

4. What practices can you build into your life to stay close to God and reduce the risk of becoming lost?

Week 12
Build Faith from Nourishing Basics

Like newborn babies, crave pure spiritual milk, so that by it you may grow up in your salvation, now that you have tasted that the Lord is good.—1 Peter 2:2-3

When babies are born, their digestive system is an "open gut"—proteins and pathogens can pass into the bloodstream through the spaces that exist between the cells of the small intestine. So, until they're around six months old, infants need to rely on milk to develop.

Starting small like this with something appropriate for where we are applies to our career or leadership. If we've never supervised anybody, we don't start out managing thousands of people. We might start with just two or three.

But it also applies to faith. When we're just starting our walk with God, we need to start with the absolute basics before we can move on to harder, more complex ideas. And sometimes, what initially seems "simple" still needs to be broken down even more before we really can digest it.

We can see this principle in John 3:16: "For God so loved the world that He gave His one and only Son, that whoever believes in Him shall not perish but have eternal life."

As a trauma survivor, I circled that verse until my feet bled. I couldn't imagine that kind of care, a Sacred Heart that sacrificial and selfless. But I *wanted* to. It held the promise that, despite everything I'd been through and felt, there was Somebody Who would not leave me by myself.

Yet, even this verse—one of the most beloved summaries of the gospel—prompts a host of questions.

Why did Jesus agree to die?

Why does God love us?

What will eternity with God be like, and why does it even matter?

Asking these kinds of questions is not a deficiency of faith God will fault us for. He gets that we'll be confused, our pea brains unable to fathom Somebody Who's always present, can't betray or lie, and has no limitations.

Rather, asking is evidence that the craving to know God is pumping through our spirit.

The very fact we ask proves that something in us longs for Him.

I learned the path: Doubt—which we inevitably bear because of our humanness and the fall in Genesis—leads to questions, questions to seeking, seeking to learning, learning to security, security to boldness, boldness to connection, connection to hope, and hope to peace.

Like any good parent, God can see our appetite and understand what we're ready for or need for balance. But we're surrounded by spiritual fast food—think scammer gurus, astrologists and mediums, or those who peddle the concept that the way to enlightenment is in finding yourself. They can seem satisfying in the moment. So, we can make mistakes and ingest what isn't good for us.

To stay well, let's intentionally adjust our palate—even if that means taking in just one verse or question at a time—so we can absorb a steady diet of the good stuff.

Challenge

This week, swap out your usual coffee or sugary soda for a healthy smoothie (dairy free is OK!). As you enjoy your treat, reflect on how much more it nourishes your body, just as God's Word nourishes and sustains your spirit.

Reflection Questions

1. What's the difference between "pure spiritual milk" and spiritual milk that's full of junk?

2. What kind of "additives" do you think mess up your spiritual taste right now?

3. How do you want "pure spiritual milk" to grow your relationship with God?

4. How can you share "pure spiritual milk" with others around you who are starving?

Week 13
Be First in Kindness, Great with God

"Then the King will say to those on his right, 'Come, you who are blessed by my Father; take your inheritance, the kingdom prepared for you since the creation of the world. For I was hungry and you gave me something to eat, I was thirsty and you invited me in, I needed clothes and you clothed me, I was sick and you looked after me, I was in prison and you came to visit me.'"—Matthew 25:34-36

When someone's nice to you, don't you want to reciprocate? Or, have you ever watched someone be nice to someone else and felt inspired to be a little kinder yourself?

A study from UCLA's Bedari Kindness Institute showed that people experience an uplifting feeling called elevation when they witness compassionate acts. The study also found that people give more to charity after watching a video of a man giving throughout the day than they do after watching a parkour video.[15]

Neuroscientifically, we naturally want to affirm and reproduce kind behavior because it reduces the risk of both physical and emotional pain.[16,17] God hardwired us to be loving to each other not only because His entire nature is peace, but also because He knows that social kindness is necessary for survival (see Week 33).

This played out for me as one of the third-party companies I worked for started to drop writers in favor of artificial intelligence. We couldn't stop the layoffs. But we all felt the unspoken undercurrent: *We have to watch out for each other, not only because it's reasonable and pragmatic, but also because it protects the art to which we assign deep spiritual and existential value.*

Each of us started sharing potential jobs with each other as we found them. We didn't all land solid work from that, but the compassion hit in a lasting way. Even months after we scattered, one of my former colleagues shared a project they thought I'd be great at.

Yet, when a lack of a desire to serve God leaves egotism unchecked, it becomes easy to sidestep our social instinct, exhibit selfishness, and believe that others don't deserve help.

It also can be difficult to care for others when we have been abused, traumatized, or left wanting. We can believe justice has been corrupted if others don't work or suffer as we do. We can get so stuck in the scarcity mindset that we get scared to give away what we have, too, even when we have more than enough.

But Jesus was clear that the way we treat other people is a crucial part of faith. By caring, we demonstrate the selfless, joy-inspired love God wants to give us.

Factors like strict agendas, pressure to deliver quickly, regulations, and social scripts can make it hard for us to be kind in the office.[18] But changes to the work environment or operational procedures can help. Identifying inefficiencies and bottlenecks, for instance, can open time for us to connect while we're not engaged in critical tasks. If we evaluate areas such as clarity of expectation and the provision of opportunity, we all can support more selfless, reciprocal compassion in our offices.

Challenge

God's love often comes to us through the hands and voices of others, and we're called to use our unique spiritual gifts to share each other's burdens and produce the fruit of the Spirit (Galatians 5:22-23, 6:2; John 13:34-35; 1 Corinthians 12). This week, become that vessel by extending intentional kindness to someone in your circle.

Identify a friend, coworker, or someone in your community you want to show more kindness to. Ask if they need anything or find out how they are holding up. Offer to perform simple acts of service, such as ordering them a meal, helping with a project, or just lending an ear to what they're experiencing.

Reflection Questions

1. How might Matthew 25:34-36 apply in the context of "non-visible" illness or emotional/spiritual need?

2. Is there a specific way of caring for others you gravitate to?

3. What are some places within your office or community where the need for care is high?

4. What barriers do you have against showing more care to those in need?

Week 14

Testify Through the End of Your Race

However, I consider my life worth nothing to me; my only aim is to finish the race and complete the task the Lord Jesus has given me— the task of testifying to the good news of God's grace.—Acts 20:24

How often have you heard a leader say it's critical to finish what you start?

Probably tons. It's not just a matter of bringing an innovative project to the market, boosting confidence with achievements, and improving the bottom line. It's also a matter of showing integrity. If we can do that, we can build the trust necessary for the relationships that let us grab success.

But when we're working for God, finishing what He assigns us is a beautiful declaration of submission and obedience. It is not about *our* success, but rather about our role and purpose in *His* success, which is to bring as many people home to Heaven as possible and to shower them in joy and love.

Many of us hear the word "testify" and clam up. We assume that "testify" means getting up and talking in front of people or doing nothing but preaching. Just about all of us fear public speaking on some level and worry we'll be rejected if we try to connect (see Week 52).

But the ways we can communicate God's grace are vast. For me, it happens through creating books like this. But as believers serving in the singular body of Christ, we express the fruit of the Spirit through all kinds of loving acts, according to the unique gifts God grants us. Maybe for you, communicating His grace means training others, mediating, or being the empathetic voice of encouragement for your organization—that's all testifying, too.

When we recognize how many ways there are to testify and contribute to God's glory, we can stop competing and give each other the space we need to be freely who God made us to be. We can accept ourselves, trust that God has properly equipped us,[19] and have courage to lead in the right place in the right way at the right time, whether that includes having a big, bold personality or not.

So, we don't have to "run" the race, per se. We can crawl, scoot, bike, skip, or even wiggle it. All that matters is that we're willing to put our number on and that we don't stop until God says we're done.

Challenge

Set yourself a distance to travel. It might be as short as the length of your room or as long as halfway around the world. Rest when needed and use any method of movement you like. But once you set your distance, don't quit—remind yourself that you are meant to run the race marked out for you (Hebrews 12:1-2; 2 Timothy 4:7). If you foresee any hurdles to completion, create an action plan for overcoming them before you start your journey.

If you want a bonus, repeat the exercise with a new distance that's a little farther than your previous one. This can help you understand that God can develop you to go further in your testimony over time.

Reflection Questions

1. Where are some places you could testify with ease right now? With difficulty? What makes them different?

2. If you had only 30 seconds to testify, what would you say?

3. What do you think is meant by "finish the race?" Have we completed the task when we testify to one person? 100? Our life ends?

4. How do you measure success along your race route?

Week 15
Embrace God's Loving Seal

*When you believed, you were marked in him with a seal, the
promised Holy Spirit, who is a deposit guaranteeing our
inheritance until the redemption of those who are God's
possession—to the praise of his glory.—Ephesians 1:13-14*

Have you ever labeled a folder or box at work? It's common
when teams collaborate, move locations, or need to archive
physical files. We give our computer files clear names, too.

What's the reason behind this labeling?

Sure, it helps us clarify what we've got and where it belongs.

But why does that matter?

Because we want to ensure no one mistakes the value of the data
or assets.

Labels have protected originality, identity, reputation,
craftsmanship, and creativity for millennia. One of the ways that
early craftsmen would identify themselves as the maker of the
product was to put a seal or brand on it. Everyone who saw the seal
knew where the product came from and who to give credit to. Our
modern logos are a continuation of this ancient practice.

Yet, sometimes, the treatment of a label can blur lines and create
confusion.

In the writing industry, bylines are labels that prove we own our
words and that we're skilled enough to be trusted with more. Yet, as
a ghostwriter, I've submitted pieces under my name and been
rejected—only to submit pieces under clients' names and be
accepted by the same outlets. I struggled to reconcile the reality that,
even though all the words were mine, the label—*not* the quality—
held the real power. I wished I had a different label, a *valuable* one. I
felt invisible, even as my words succeeded without me.

The gospel, however, tells me I have a seal of infinite worth
(Ephesians 1:13, 4:30; 2 Corinthians 1:21-22; Revelation 7:2-3, 14:1).

So do you.

When we come to believe in Christ, we are labeled in an unmistakable way through the Holy Spirit. God has only to glance at us to know that we are His workmanship and will forever have value. The seal cannot be broken or faked, and it entitles us to everything He offers.

God's seal becomes visible through our words and behavior. If we want to know who truly belongs to God, we must look at their fruit—that is, the evidence of their words and actions (Matthew 7:15-20). Fruit isn't just what's on a metrics sheet. It's the character, love, and transformation that flow from a Spirit-led life.

The visibility of God's seal allows others to be drawn to God through us, and it protects us by revealing who can be a trustworthy companion in faith. Be intentional about speaking and acting in a way that puts your seal on full display, and look for the seal of God on others to make a wise call about how to interact.

Challenge

In honor of God's seal, make some sugar cookies (or a diabetic-friendly alternative). Before you pop the cookies in the oven, use a fork or other kitchen utensil to put marks on your treats. Note that, although baking changes the cookies, it doesn't remove the seal. In the same way, the seal of the Holy Spirit that exists on you doesn't go away when you go through tough stuff that transforms you.

If you want to go even further, share some of your cookies with others. Just about everybody likes a sweet treat, and it's a simple way to witness and connect with authenticity and love as the only agendas.

Reflection Questions

1. What do people say or do that makes it clear to you they have God's seal?

2. Can anything erase the mark God made on you that verifies you're His?

3. How is the mark of God like the signature of a proud artist (Genesis 1:31; Isaiah 49:16)? Have you ever considered God's pride in you before?

4. In Exodus 12:13-28, God sees the blood on the doorposts and passes over the homes of His people. How does this physical mark point to the seal we now receive through Jesus' sacrifice on the cross?

Week 16
Feed Your Spiritual Hunger

Jesus answered, "It is written: 'Man shall not live on bread alone,
but on every word that comes from the mouth of God.'"
—Matthew 4:4

Even though many of us could do a little better about stepping away from our desks to enjoy our meals, most of us are pretty good at listening to our hunger cues. Probably everybody anticipates Taco Tuesday with a little glee and drooling. We cater work meals and have fundraising dinners because food's such a good, basic motivator, too.

But all of us have spiritual hunger, as well. We want to understand what we're here for, see meaning, and connect to something bigger than we are. We want to feel peace tickle and relax our souls.

This spiritual hunger has a purpose. It draws us closer to God—the only Being who can satisfy the craving—and transforms us to be closer to His image (see Weeks 12 and 20).

Yet, many of us end up in spiritual starvation. We tell ourselves we can wait to pray until after work, but when we get home, we're so tired or distracted we don't say a single word to God. Convinced we don't have 10 minutes to read the Word for comfort and wisdom, we read our social media feeds for an hour, hoping to discover Some Faster New Hack to relieve our suffering.

Worse, we try to satisfy our spiritual hunger with junk food from the Devil's quick delivery—addictions and materialism, endless mantras that don't stop the fear we don't matter, and winning achievement after achievement.

What would our lives and businesses look like, though, if we responded to our spiritual hunger with the same urgency as our physical hunger?

We talk a ton about physically taking care of ourselves so we have the bodily energy necessary to perform well. But life is as spiritually exhausting as it is physically demanding. The only way we'll get through it and serve God well is if we take the spiritual nourishment we need to put Satan and all his little cronies in the proper place. They are constantly feeding on the pain they inflict. If we want to beat them, we can't skip the meals God has ready for us.

Challenge

Habit stacking or bundling—linking new habits to existing ones—is a proven strategy for adopting new behaviors. To integrate the idea into your spiritual growth, each time you have a meal or snack, instead of eating on autopilot or scrolling social media, access your Bible or a Christian book, video, audiobook, or podcast. Read, watch, or listen as you enjoy your food. Take a few notes about how you feel, what you learned, or questions you have.

At the end of your session, thank God for taking care of you physically and spiritually. Because meals and snacks are something you must accommodate every day, attaching them to the Word ensures that you regularly connect with God.

Reflection Questions

1. Do you have barriers keeping you from feeling hungry for God? If so, what are they?

2. What does Matthew 4:4 suggest about getting into the Word or praying, given that we need many meals in our lives?

3. What is the verse you consider to be most nourishing for you?

4. How might you increase the spiritual nourishment you get from God?

Week 17
Wield God's Love, Trust His Justice

Do not say, "I will repay evil"; wait for the Lord, and he will deliver you.—Proverbs 20:22

As professionals, we're incredibly good at seeing competitors as enemies and painting the corporate environment as dog-eat-dog (see Week 10). In fact, as part of competitive intelligence, businesses routinely take part in "war games." During these events, the point is to try to understand other companies in the market to be able to defeat them. It's possible to approach this task focusing more on the "game" part than the "war" part.

But all too often, we go in with an attitude of annihilation at all costs. Trusting our own assessment of what fair is, we skip mercy and worry only about our own bottom line. With this approach, we believe that life—and profits—would be significantly better if the competing companies didn't exist.

Even if it is never the case that we need to become allies with others in the future, having competitors around by nature forces us to be more mindful. We are better challenged to evaluate our products, services, and strategies.

In the end, this motivates us to do better. When we do better, customers notice, buy, and stay loyal. They notice, too, when we have an attitude of integrity and kindness where others do not.

This is why asking God to bless other companies or personal rivals, trusting the fullness of His justice, and breaking the cycle of retribution benefits us.

Vengeance is God's (Deuteronomy 32:35; Romans 12:9), and King Solomon—the wisest man in history—paints a clear picture of love as a powerful spiritual tool of defeat: "If your enemy is hungry, give him food to eat; if he is thirsty, give him water to drink. In doing this you will heap burning coals on his head, and the Lord will reward you" (Proverbs 25:21-22).

In God's economy, excellence and compassion aren't opposites—they're teammates. Instead of trying to get even or getting distracted by petty tactics or politics, let's focus on being at the top of our game.

Challenge

Make a list of your personal or corporate competitors. Pray for each of them in a specific way. You don't have to abandon healthy ambition or pray that they succeed more than you. But you *can* pray that they act with integrity, experience the love of Jesus, avoid unnecessary suffering, engage fairly with you, or even grow strong enough to present you with a worthy challenge.

Praying this way trains you to let go of bitterness, see others as fellow image-bearers, and place your trust in God's justice and provision, not just your own strength (see Weeks 3, 6, and 20).

Reflection Questions

1. What makes it difficult to forgive or pray for enemies?

2. Can you identify a time when you thought someone was against you? What happened? What might you have done differently?

3. What enemies did Jesus have? Why?

4. What behaviors would make you consider someone an enemy—and how might you respond in a way that protects your values while inviting reconciliation?

Week 18

Lose the Mask, Show Who You Are

"But what about you?" he asked. "Who do you say that I am?"
Simon Peter answered, "You are the Messiah, the Son of the living
God."—Matthew 16:15-16

Right now, in the corporate world, there's a massive emphasis on being authentic and transparent.

Many of us find this to be extremely challenging, even so. We wear masks over our thinking and way of being, afraid that if we reveal ourselves completely, we'll be judged harshly and fail.

For a long time, this hindered my ability to testify for God (see Week 14). I didn't think people would respond well if I shared the wisdom or deep emotions I had, *especially* in the office where the authority to apply knowledge often is seen as earned rather than gifted (see Week 45), and where—despite the popular emphasis on emotional intelligence—feelings can be seen as speed bumps against pragmatic action. I buried what I thought and quieted convictions I knew were true under a mountain of people-pleasing, and I refused to share anything about my personal life that might rock the boat.

But God is completely truthful all the time (Titus 1:2; Numbers 23:19). He might not reveal certain things until the timing is right or we can better understand, but He does not hide His true character. In the same way, Jesus—the way and the truth and the life (John 14:6)—behaved with a beautiful consistency of integrity that made His disciples certain He was the Son of God.

You might be at a place in your life where you are still trying to figure out who you are and what you can bring to the table. That's OK! On that journey, seek to know more of Who God is, because you are in His image (see Week 20). In finding parts of Him, you will also find parts of yourself.

As you explore how to reveal who you are, be encouraged by the fact redeemed corporate authenticity can have many faces—the pastor who confesses burnout, the manager who makes a public apology, or the entrepreneur who walks away from a deal rather than water down their mission. Leaders like Truett Cathy (Chick-fil-A), David Green (Hobby Lobby), and Mary Kay Ash (Mary Kay Cosmetics) reveal that self-honesty toward faith can be a cornerstone component of operational success, not a liability.

Recall, too, that part of your identity is to be a sister or brother of Jesus, a joint heir to the kingdom of Heaven. This is a role you can never be fired or removed from. Take heart from that, but be willing to take up the responsibilities that come with it, too.

Challenge

Look through your Bible and investigate all the ways people describe God. Reread some of the stories that are familiar to you and see if you can pull out the more subtle aspects of God's wisdom and nature that you might have missed. The more shades you see in His character, the deeper understanding you'll have of who you are supposed to be, what you're meant to model in your faith, and how Who He is influences your trust, worship, and decisions.

Additionally, keep a journal for a few days and reflect on the roles that you have and how you view yourself in them. How might God's nature influence those roles? Ask at least one other person to do the same thing about you. Then compare notes to see if you really have a good sense of who you are.

Reflection Questions

1. What does it mean that Jesus is God's Son? How does His crucifixion deepen that meaning?

2. Accepting that God's love and grace are constant even when we struggle to recognize our worth, who are you without God? With Him?

3. Who do you want to be in the future as a Christian?

4. Which people do you connect to as a believer? How might that shape who you become?

Week 19
Share Jesus, Lose Nothing

But we have this treasure in jars of clay to show that this all-surpassing power is from God and not from us.—2 Corinthians 4:7

Have you ever gotten a certificate or work award? Maybe a plaque with your name etched on it?

You probably prized those things and saw them as treasures within your career.

In Jesus' time, people had treasures, too—precious metals and coins, jewelry, important documents, or even beads or bones. But instead of putting those valuables in a safe like we do today, they stored them in jars for protection. In times of unrest, they'd bury the jars to make sure the treasures weren't stolen (Jeremiah 32:14; Matthew 13:44).[20,21]

In this context, when the apostle Paul speaks in 2 Corinthians 4:7, he explains that each of us is a vessel, a jar of clay literally formed by God from the dust of the Earth. And as believers, we hold a treasure in our hearts that's far more valuable than anything we could earn by our own merit—the knowledge of Jesus Christ. Because we're only clay, when God uses us to share the Good News, that power is not from us, but from God.

The knowledge of Jesus, which God has mercifully placed in us, is a treasure not only because it reconnects us to the Creator, but also because it can be given away to others. The miracle within this is that, in sharing the treasure of Jesus, we never see our portion of that treasure depleted. We can share Him yet never lose what He has measured out for us.

Challenge

Find a nice journal, binder, or notebook. Tape or glue pictures of yourself and your loved ones on it as a reminder that the treasure of knowing Jesus is meant to be written in our hearts and lives. Then use the journal, binder, or notebook to take notes when you go to church or read your Bible.

Alternatively, get a simple, inexpensive clay pot. Write a Scripture verse you want to memorize on a Post-it and place it on the jar until you've committed it to memory. When you know the verse, put the Post-it in the pot and write a new verse to memorize. If you like, paint 2 Corinthians 4:7 on the pot.

Reflection Questions

1. How does the knowledge of Jesus inside of you improve your life? Complicate it?

2. In what ways can we place the knowledge of Jesus inside of others?

3. What do you know about Jesus that makes you feel most full?

4. What might deplete or increase our fullness as a vessel of God?

Week 20
Imitate the One True Teacher

Then God said, "Let us make mankind in our image, in our likeness, so that they may rule over the fish of the sea and the birds in the sky, over the livestock and all the wild animals, and over all the creatures that move along the ground." —Genesis 1:26

We often use Genesis 1:26 to conceptualize the physical image of God: If we are made in God's image, then God must look like us. After all, it doesn't make much sense that a creature made in the image of a cow would look like a raccoon for some reason. We can see our compulsion to assume God's appearance is similar to ours in how Jesus is portrayed in art across cultures.[22]

But Scripture also shows that, much like the shapeshifting Queen Watevra Wa'Nabi (Whatever I Wanna Be) in *The Lego Movie 2*, God can take a variety of forms whenever He likes (e.g., a pillar of fire, Exodus 13:21-22).

So, what happens if we interpret Genesis 1:26 solely in the context of character, values, and behavior?

The Bible leaves no question that we are meant to try to copy God's attitude, beliefs, and way of behaving. In Matthew 5:48, Jesus gives instruction to "Be perfect, therefore, as your heavenly Father is perfect."

In this sense, our assignment to rule over and subdue the Earth reflects the larger work God does through all creation. He rules over everything but has given us a small portion to be lesser masters and mistresses over. If we want to do a good job of managing what He's given us, then we must look at how He manages everything else.

Yet, instead of trying to create an image based on God, we often copy what famous leaders do—sometimes even down to wearing the same hairstyle—in the hope we'll become successful like they are.

God can and does put others in our lives who can improve us toward the plans He has for us. But turning ourselves into clones erases the beautiful uniqueness God intends and celebrates in us. It is not mentorship, which is a healthy relationship between two people offering customized, well-intentioned guidance and support. And mentorship, which is more about skills, knowledge, or professional development in a specific area, is not discipleship, which means that we deeply integrate what we learn from the teacher into who we are and how we live, transforming ourselves on a core values level to a completely different way of life.

There is only One True Teacher. We're made to carry His image, not anyone else's. Let's not substitute or misplace our discipleship.

Challenge

Make a list of the physical, behavioral, and character traits you believe God has, based on Scripture. Then make a similar list for yourself. There will inevitably be a gap—you're only human. But reflect on what might be causing the distance. This acknowledgement opens the door to repentance and honest growth.

Next, go back and highlight the positive qualities in your list (see Week 4). The point isn't to ignore your flaws—it's to remind you that God's presence is already at work in you. The more clearly you see the ways He has shaped you and the gifts He's entrusted to you, the more motivation you'll have to keep running the race of testimony we're all called to (see Week 14).

Reflection Questions

1. How do you usually picture God in your head? Why?

2. In what ways do you struggle with seeing yourself as reflecting God? In what ways do you do OK?

3. What do you think are the most important elements of God to copy? Why?

4. What are some small steps you could take this week to shape yourself more toward God's character?

Week 21
Respond Slowly and Build Space

Do not be quick with your mouth, do not be hasty in your heart to utter anything before God. God is in heaven and you are on earth, so let your words be few.—Ecclesiastes 5:2

If we all had a quarter for every time we've heard that business is fast-paced, everybody'd probably be able to retire on a white-sand island. As technology advances and breaks down global barriers, the pace is getting only faster. We're warned of that with the same frequency we check our email (in fact, the warnings can come in an email).

The pressure is heavy to respond as quickly as possible. We don't always feel like there is time to pause and let our emotions cool. But if we move too fast, we can say and do less-than-stellar things that not only hurt our career or business, but that dishonor God.

What's a professional to do?

Wherever you can, be an advocate for space. Space to breathe, conceptualize, compare, and weigh. Space to ask questions—*especially the ones that are the scariest to ask* (see Week 12).[23] Build this space into your habits, such as going for a quick walk around the building when you feel angry. Integrate it into your workflows, such as giving people on your team more time in meetings so they can properly process and respond to what's going on. *Remember: We have enough time when we properly prioritize.*

As you advocate, think through the potential ramifications of what you would say. The adage of "Is it helpful, kind, or necessary?" can provide a good, basic guardrail by which you can self-evaluate your thoughts (see Week 5). We often apply this question to improve our interactions with people. But if you add "to God" to the inquiry, you might be surprised at how it changes the rationale and energy for your next move.

Challenge

Any time you are in a conversation this week, practice restraint by not formulating your response while the other person is still speaking. Instead, give yourself a second or two before you respond. It's OK to ask for a moment to reflect. If you get non-urgent texts or emails, wait 5 to 10 minutes before you send your response.

Remember: Delay doesn't mean indifference. It centers you in attentiveness rather than reaction. Controlling your tongue in this way models Christ's wisdom, timing, intentionality, and emotional maturity in conversation (Matthew 27:12-14; John 8:6-7, 19:9-11; Luke 20:1-8; Mark 12:13-17; Isaiah 53:7).

Reflection Questions

1. What are some of the benefits of practicing good active listening and getting picky about what you say?

2. How does it feel to wait longer than usual to respond? How do you think others might feel when they see you slowing down and choosing your words with care?

3. What do you think pressures us to be quick with our mouths even outside the corporate world?

4. Have you ever said or done something you wished God hadn't heard or seen? What happened? What would you say or do differently today?

Week 22
Climb Through Humility

Do nothing out of selfish ambition or vain conceit. Rather, in humility value others above yourselves.—Philippians 2:3

Let's be frank: Nobody likes to deal with an egotistical jerk who's only out to crush everybody else under their heel.

At the same time, Western culture very much connects ambition in a positive way to grit, perseverance, autonomy, individualism, and self-sufficiency, to the degree that we can struggle to consider how ambition might ever be toxic.[24] *Healthy* ambition, which is sustainable and focused, means we're likely to dream, innovate, and push hard when things get tough. That's what champions do.

But what is the purpose of business?

It's not to line our pockets, procure a corner office, or get fame and power for ourselves.

The purpose of business is to serve.

A million companies can serve in a million different ways. But because every organization exists to serve others instead of ourselves, humility isn't just a soft skill. It's a spiritual mandate, foundational to leadership in any form.

Jesus explains that humility and servant leadership connect to our position with God: "Instead, whoever wants to become great among you must be your servant, and whoever wants to be first must be slave of all. For even the Son of Man did not come to be served, but to serve, and to give his life as a ransom for many" (Mark 10:44-45). The more we push and hustle to reach the top by asserting our own place and entitlement, the more we slide to the bottom.

Unfortunately, many people look out for number one and believe the organization is meant to serve *them.*

I once miscalculated with a potential client this way. They were looking for someone to do some social media work for them and needed a simple solution. But I built a larger proposal, chasing the freedom and autonomy the extra income promised. Instead of focusing on what they needed, I focused on what I wanted.

Needless to say, they didn't sign a contract with me.

I realize now that I wasn't pitching my service in a way that built the potential client up—I was drawing blueprints for a house I hadn't even asked God if I should build.

This doesn't mean we can't enjoy some rewards as we work. It just means that rewards are a privilege instead of a right, and that others can enjoy them even as we do.

As we approach our to-do list today, let's not worry about our advancement or paycheck. Instead, let's worry about whether we're willing to sacrifice and tap every skill we have on behalf of others. When we lead in humility this way, we don't just strengthen careers—we build the kind of legacy God honors.

Challenge

Take stock of your coworkers throughout the week. Notice the tasks they do well—especially ones they handle more effectively than you. Acknowledge these strengths and thank your coworkers for them specifically.

If appropriate, ask how they developed those skills or what motivates them. Is there anything they could teach you directly? Let your curiosity and gratitude become a bridge of connection and humility.

Reflection Questions

1. Why is it important to recognize the strengths and talents in others that exceed our own (1 Corinthians 12)?

2. What is the difference between humility and shame? How does that influence your view of weaknesses?

3. Think back to a time when you acted with selfish ambition or vain conceit (we're all human!). If it gave you any good feelings or results, did those last?

4. What are your biggest ambitions right now? How can you pursue them without falling into pride or comparison?

Week 23
Grind Down Your False Idols

Where then are the gods you made for yourselves? Let them come if they can save you when you are in trouble! For you, Judah, have as many gods as you have towns.—Jeremiah 2:28

A striking part of Israel's story is how often they made gods for themselves, missing how that reversed the whole power dynamic of divine creation. We can't be both creator and created.

Part of Israel's struggle was rooted in repeated exposure to the polytheism of Egypt and surrounding cultures. Today, it's just as easy to grow lukewarm in faith simply because we're surrounded by so many alternatives. We might not fashion a golden calf the way the Israelites did (Exodus 32), but we do fashion golden bank accounts, social media profiles, or coveted speaking engagements.

Like the gods the prophet Jeremiah condemned, these modern gods won't save us. They don't deserve our worship. That's why Jesus didn't call out to money on the cross.

But I know firsthand how seductive these false gods can *feel*.

When my children were younger, it seemed prudent to make them wait as I spent yet another hour on the computer to build a more stable career. It wasn't until I saw the toll it took—their struggle to trust that I would truly be present and care—that I realized I'd built an altar along the horribly wrong path. I had to confront that *idols can show up even among our best intentions*.

Excelling in anything—even a career—requires us to recognize where and how we've built false gods that pull our focus from Jesus. It's tempting to resist that recognition because it admits our faith has been imperfect. But acknowledging where we have strayed allows us to ask God for forgiveness and to course correct.

This kind of pivot ought not to make us wail and gnash our teeth. *Whenever God calls us to repentance, it is not to leave us drenched in guilt and shame, staring with embarrassment at the floor, but rather to offer an opportunity to surrender and exchange the weight of sin for freedom. This is a fantastic privilege, an invitation to happiness and celebration!*[25]

Just as God was merciful as Israel danced around their gold, so too, will He be merciful when we grind our own calf to dust. And when we return to Him, we won't have to settle for scraps—we'll have a feast topped off with a full measure of joy (Luke 15:11-31; John 17:13).

Challenge

Research some of the gods that led Israel away from the Lord (e.g., Baal, Asherah, Molech). What desires or fears did these gods appeal to? Then reflect honestly and make a list of the elements—habits, people, systems, goals—you've been tempted to treat as gods in your own life. Consider what they promise you—and what they cost.

Reflection Questions

1. Making a god of something doesn't happen overnight. What do you think are the stages of this gradual process?

2. What are some modern gods you see people around you prioritizing or trusting in more than God? How do you recognize those patterns?

3. What strategies can you use to avoid making something into a god and worshipping it?

4. What internal longings or external pressures make you (or others) vulnerable to idolizing something other than God?

Week 24
Be Ready for God's Interruption

After this, Jesus went out and saw a tax collector by the name of Levi sitting at his tax booth. "Follow me," Jesus said to him, and Levi got up, left everything and followed him.—Luke 5:27-28

We've probably all experienced it at least once—the supervisor interrupts what we're doing, tells us to come *right this second*, and walks away expecting us to be on their heels.

Maybe the reason they call us away is an emergency. Maybe it isn't. But in that scenario, we probably feel a little torn, knowing we should go but irritated by the fact they broke our focus.

Jesus interrupted Levi with this kind of urgent directive. But unlike us in our workplace moments, Levi might have felt only gratitude.

During that time, people abhorred tax collectors, similar to how many Americans don't like Internal Revenue Service agents today.[26] Rome—an empire the Jews saw as oppressive—allowed the local men they hired to pocket anything they collected beyond the tax fees. Many intentionally overcharged people to grow rich.

It's not clear from Scripture whether Levi really was a crook or people just thought he was. Either way, the respect people gave him likely was low.

Yet, there Jesus—Teacher of Teachers—was, promising to teach *him*. To be a *friend*.

In that moment, Levi might have realized he was losing nothing by repenting and walking away from his table (see Week 23).

Most professionals aren't corrupt. But many of us climb the ladder only to realize that people assume we are. It's also common to achieve financial success only to find that, as we put in more hours, it's harder to connect to anybody. That disconnect can leave us wondering whether what we've built is worth staying around for.

As you sit at your table today, how tied to it are you? Does Jesus offer more than it does?

If the thought of leaving what you have fills you with anxiety, remember: God never calls us away from something without leading us into something better. He can "meet all of your needs according to the riches of his glory in Christ Jesus" (Philippians 4:19), and *complete* satisfaction is a pretty good deal.

Challenge

Have someone you trust set a series of timers during your non-work hours on your phone or another device. Alternatively, arrange for them to send you texts.

The plot twist? You can't know in advance when those timers or texts will hit.

When the timers activate, being mindful of safety and respectful of previous commitments, drop whatever it is you are doing for at least 10 minutes. Use the time to listen to a Christian podcast or streaming station, read the Bible or other Christian content, or pray.

For a deeper variation, drop your regular rhythm for an entire day or weekend to attend a Christian seminar or retreat.

After each interruption, reflect on whether you feel more grounded, focused, or open when you return to your work.

We don't know when Jesus will collect us the way He came for Levi. But we can practice letting go of worldly distractions so we learn to respond without hesitation when the invitation comes.

Reflection Questions

1. What other groups in Jesus' time were considered socially corrupt, outcast, or spiritually unworthy—like the tax collectors?

2. Have you ever felt hated or had conflict just for trying to do your job?

3. What does Luke 5:27-28 suggest about who qualifies to follow Jesus? Why does that matter?

4. How does Levi's background and reputation compare to the other disciples Jesus called? What does this tell us about the kind of people Jesus chooses?

Week 25

Accept the Assignment, No Matter the Rank

Jesus did not let him, but said, "Go home to your own people and tell them how much the Lord has done for you, and how he has had mercy on you."—Mark 5:19

In the 1998 comedy *The Waterboy*, Bobby Boucher Jr. (Adam Sandler) sits on the sidelines while the men around him play football. His whole job? Make sure everybody has water. People make fun of him as he does it.

Later, Bobby proves he has ridiculous tackling skills. But you might argue his initial job was the most important one of all, because the players' ability to perform depended on whether they were properly hydrated.

There's a famous story of former American President John F. Kennedy visiting a NASA space center.[27] The President asked a janitor what he did for NASA. The janitor responded that he was helping to put a man on the moon.

There was truth in the janitor's words. In his own waterboy way, he provided a foundation for the NASA personnel, ensuring they had the safe, clean environment necessary to develop and carry out their historic launch.

You might have had a Bobby Boucher moment in your office, assigned work that felt "meaningless" or beneath you. But *no roles are inconsequential*, regardless of whether you are talking about your organization or working for Jesus.

The man healed of demons likely saved many people in his community by doing what Jesus told him to do. Those people would not have known the Lord if the man had traveled with Jesus like the other disciples.

Like Bobby Boucher and the NASA janitor, we're connected to a larger purpose. It's not up to us to choose the responsibilities God will assign to us. What *is* up to us is whether we accept the assignment we're given and take pride in whatever part we play.

If God asks you to be a waterboy, don't worry about the linebackers and quarterbacks. Just go make sure you have enough cups.

Challenge

What has God done for you in the past day, week, month, or year? Have you shared it with others?

Find someone who doesn't yet know how God blessed you and tell them your story. You can share your testimony online, but remember how Jesus instructed the man healed of demons to speak about Him in his own hometown. The greatest impact often happens not on stages or big platforms, but in one-on-one conversations with those we know and love.

Reflection Questions

1. What do you think life was like for the man with the demons before Jesus healed him? After?

2. How do you think the man with the demons felt when he wasn't allowed to come with Jesus?

3. Have you ever been assigned to do a job that was different than you originally wanted? If so, what was the outcome?

4. What does Mark 5:19 teach you about the difference between doing what *you* want and doing what *God* calls you to do?

Week 26
Ditch the Bias, Pick Up Grace

Be wise in the way you act toward outsiders; make the most of every opportunity. Let your conversation be always full of grace, seasoned with salt, so that you may know how to answer everyone.—Colossians 4:5-6

In 2022, researchers from the University of Essex attempted to unpack stereotypes around boredom.[28] *What makes a typically boring person? How do people react to them?*

The study revealed that we see some professions—e.g., data analysis—as more boring than others. We also tend to avoid and dislike others in those professions.

Our job biases aren't harmless. They shape how we treat others and can lead us to be unkind. That's reason for pause, given that all professions are economically linked and that the way we interact has a bearing on spiritual, mental, and emotional health.

We have the power to challenge biases. And whenever we reach out to others, we have an opportunity not just to share ourselves, which can help us feel connected and confident, but also to recognize and celebrate who others are. This is the salt or seasoning Paul describes, and it's not just kindness. It's the presence of Christ in us, making every word we speak a chance to reflect His grace, joy, and creativity. We don't need to add a lot to someone's life for it to make a difference.

Sometimes, we close tighter than clams, get misinterpreted as bores, or are unkind because we genuinely don't know we can trust other people or don't believe we have anything worth sharing. Patience from others is the ingredient that allows us to push past this inner guard. It might help our careers or other areas of our lives in the long run, but more importantly, it opens space for blessing: What really gives real meaning to our interaction opportunities is making sure that the people we meet know they are loved by God—and that their words, too, can carry His goodwill into the world.

Challenge

For several days, try cooking without seasoning or salt. Does your food taste blander? Flatter? Reflect on what life feels like when you can't show your true self or encouragement is missing.

Then, have a flavorful meal. Notice the difference. Does it taste better? Do you enjoy it more? Consider how much more satisfying life becomes when we show up with presence, purpose, peace, and passion.

Alternatively, come up with a list of phrases, actions, or strategies you can use to add flavor to your interactions, such as offering affirmations, sharing words of truth and hope, or asking thoughtful questions.[29]

Reflection Questions

1. How might we use our individual spiritual gifts to add flavor to the world aside from in conversation?

2. In what other ways did people use salt in the Bible (e.g., Ezekiel 16:4; Leviticus 2:13)?

3. Why did Jesus refer to believers as "the salt of the Earth" in Matthew 5:13-16? How does that connect to Colossians 4:5-6?

4. Who do you think would benefit from your salt the most?

Week 27
Starve Gossip, Fuel Peace

Without wood a fire goes out; without a gossip a quarrel dies down. — *Proverbs 26:20*

In a study from Harvard Business School, researchers found that, when 3G technology came into an area, the use of social media went up. As social media use went up, companies behaved better.[30] The study suggested that leaders understood how quickly word could travel about what they did and were making intentional efforts to avoid being seen badly.

The HBS study shows that the way we connect and share information potentially can provide a wide, democratic level of accountability for individuals and businesses. That's assuming, of course, that what we share is based on truth.

That's often not what happens. We can gather around the water cooler to whisper-complain without having all the pieces of the puzzle. Mob mentality can kick in and create unnecessary conflicts and fear.

It's not always in our power to confirm or deny what's being said. We can lack information others have, or we might not be authorized to say anything. Sometimes, we can get more facts and get the permission we'd need to talk to others about the situation.

But underneath Proverbs 26:20 sits the idea of autonomy. We can choose to spread what we've heard and fan the flames—*or* we can choose to be peacemakers through silence.

To quiet the room and carry the weight of reconciliation was Jesus' goal as Caiaphas and Pontius Pilate questioned Him (Matthew 26:63, 27:12-14; Mark 14:61, 15:3-5; Luke 23:9). In deliberately not engaging those who insisted He answer, He showed purposeful restraint and authority, ensuring a complete end not just to the immediate conflict, but also to every pain and disharmony the world ever would suffer.

The business world masterfully trains us to respond. But when the heat is at our feet, sometimes the loudest thing we can say is nothing.

Challenge

When you interact with others who are gossiping, do your best to appear neutral to whatever they say. Many people gossip because they find it rewarding to provoke emotional reactions in others. So, if you maintain a "stone face," you'll remove some of the motivation they have for continuing the conversation.

If the gossip continues, ask for evidence or sources supporting their claims, and be prepared to offer evidence for your own words. Ask thoughtful questions, too. You'll usually either understand their thinking better—which has empathetic value—or reach a point where they withdraw because they can't substantiate what they're saying.

But if the gossiper *still* won't quit, politely express that you're uncomfortable continuing the conversation. If possible, excuse yourself.

Any of these options run some risk that the gossiper might become hostile. But you don't have to return hostility for hostility—choose with intentionality to turn the other cheek (Luke 6:29). When you have a choice between pleasing people and pleasing God, always choose God.

Reflection Questions

1. In what situations do you or those around you face the strongest temptation to gossip? Why do you think that is?

2. What emotions or reactions do you notice in yourself when you hear gossip? How do those feelings affect you?

3. How could asking yourself, "Is it truthful, kind, or necessary?" help you resist the urge to gossip (see Week 21)?

4. Is there someone in your life who tends to gossip that you could approach with compassion and accountability? How might you begin that conversation?

Week 28
Transform Through the Mercy of God

Therefore, if anyone is in Christ, the new creation has come: The old has gone, the new is here!—2 Corinthians 5:17

In the corporate environment, we see reinventing our business, products, or services as essential to survival—innovate or die.

God has a similar view about us. But unlike companies that innovate from a fear of obsolescence, God reinvents, changes, and improves us because He's driven by love. He cares too much to leave us where we can't reach our deepest potential. He's not reacting to market forces, but rather building the healed, Spirit-powered people He saw in His heart. It's vision-orientation and completion at its finest (see Weeks 14 and 37).

Our successful transformation isn't in our control, and we can't earn our newness by our own merit. No matter how much personal development or training we do on our own, it takes the mercy of God to break the barriers of the heart and open us to be spiritually different (see Weeks 2 and 46).

That's where Jesus comes in.

When we have faith in Him, our old behaviors and ways of thinking atrophy. Our attitude, willingness to listen, and ability to serve all shift, not just for improvement's sake, but so we can participate more fully in God's mission.

These are positive things. But be prepared: Growth and grief can run along parallel tracks.

When my husband and I moved to Minnesota, I had to come to terms with the fact that, despite my dual degrees in oboe and vocal performance, a full music career simply wasn't in the cards for me. I turned to writing without fully understanding at the time how God was preparing me to communicate messages to help people reclaim lost joy. I've accepted that mission now, but there are still moments where my fingers run over the piano keys with a nearly unbearable sadness.

You might occasionally miss the way things were or wish you could reconnect with people from your past. You're allowed to grieve the loss of paths you might have taken but didn't. Give yourself some time to lean into this grief and process it. In doing so, you make space to release everything you grieve for, which will enable you to commit to the new life God is giving you (see Week 50).

Challenge

Come up with a way to repurpose an old project, such as turning a paper you wrote into a video or social media post. As you try to reinvent your previous work or belongings, do your best not to let your bias about how things "should" be get in the way of your creativity. Have patience with the transformation process, too, just as God's work in us is lovingly persistent.

Reflection Questions

1. Do you feel like you are different than you used to be? If so, in what ways have you changed?

2. What does 2 Corinthians 5:17 imply about holding onto guilt, shame, loss, or other negative elements in your life?

3. What do you think you are supposed to look like and do as a new creation?

4. How do you experience transformation with God—as a continual journey or a single event?

Week 29
Speak Through God's Power

But Moses said to the Lord, "Since I speak with faltering lips, why would Pharaoh listen to me?"—Exodus 6:30

For decades, psychologists have named public speaking as one of our biggest fears. The concept goes that we're wary of public speaking—even in everyday interactions—because, deep down, we think we might be ostracized and rejected if we mess the communication up (see Week 52).[31] We subconsciously connect the anticipated loss of inclusion with a loss of safety, which turns the "simple" act of communication into an existential crisis.

The fact that good communication ties to money might pile on even more pressure: The Society for Human Resource Management (SHRM) reports that a small business can lose an average of $420,000 every year due to poor communications. A larger business could see a loss of $62.4 million annually.[32] With business going global, the expectation to respond efficiently, effectively, and eloquently never has been higher.

Moses found himself facing the high stakes of communication when God appeared to him in a burning bush with a call to lead the Israelites out of Egypt (Exodus 3-4).

Some theologians suggest that Moses might have expressed the words in Exodus 6:30 because he suffered from a speech disability (e.g., a stutter), despite the excellent education he likely had as the adopted son of the Pharaoh's daughter.

But Moses was as much a murderer as he was a prince of Egypt. He fled Egypt after he killed an Egyptian taskmaster in defense of an Israelite slave. His fear of retribution from the Pharaoh might have prompted him to try to find any excuse he could—including a lack of eloquence—to avoid returning to Egypt.

These scenarios aren't necessarily mutually exclusive. But from the very beginning of his interaction with God, Moses used his alleged poor speaking skills as a rationale to avoid accepting God's call.

What did God do in response to Moses' lamentations?

He didn't sit in the bush and tell Moses, "Oh, you're totally eloquent! You'll be awesome!"

Instead, he reminded Moses that *He* had the greater power and would help Moses speak.

God's call often feels intimidating precisely because it pushes us into public faith, regardless of what mode of testimony He might give to us (see Week 14). But when we are anxious that we won't communicate well, God is willing to give us the right words at the right time.

Those words don't only convey God's message. They also protect us when we face those who could do us harm—we might not face a Pharaoh, but we might go head-to-head with malicious competitors or critics who threaten to cut our dreams off at the knees.

What's more, just as God gave Moses the ability to make a snake of his rod, God is willing to equip us with other power to ensure people believe what we say.

What has God asked you to speak—and what excuse might you be giving Him?

As we prepare our email or step toward the podium, there is strength in unequivocally knowing we are God's bullhorn, carried not by ego, but by Spirit-led conviction. The words are His. Our duty is merely to amplify them.

Challenge

Taking care to be safe and wise about the information you share online, record a short video message that is important and authentic for you. Don't edit it, as perfection can make a message seem too "plastic" or fake. Post the clip to your social media platforms or website.

Repeat this process each day through the week. Take stock of the thoughts that happen before and after you post, as they can give you clues about how you feel about yourself, your skills and talents, and your relationships.

At the end of the week, assess whether posting feels a little more comfortable than when you started. Even if you're still nervous, remember that *God's protection and outcomes are not dependent on your feelings*—He can help you win no matter what your emotions might be. Congratulate yourself for increasing your visibility and ask God for continued courage.

Reflection Questions

1. Have you ever had a time in your life when you let fear hold back your message, or when you thought your communication skills weren't good enough to get a good result?

2. Noting how Aaron served as a practical, trustworthy ally and spokesperson for Moses, how might finding a helper of your own encourage you as you try to communicate for yourself and God?

3. Which people—e.g., mentors, friends, pastors—can you ask to support you in your communication endeavors?

4. What does the fact Moses succeeded despite his apprehensions suggest you should do when you feel called (but scared) to speak for God?

Week 30
Submit Instead of Worrying

Can any one of you by worrying add a single hour to your life?
—Matthew 6:27

Professionals are fantastic worriers. We're trained to look for potential problems, be mindful of the trends around them, and masterfully manage risks. Even as entry-level workers, we can worry about whether we're learning and advancing fast enough, and imposter syndrome is based on the worry that others will discover our self-perceived incompetence or inexperience.

At the heart of worry are basic fears, such as losing what we need to physically survive. These fears are normal. And given how the corporate world encourages us to think about worst-case scenarios, our instinct might be to dismiss Matthew 6:27 and feel like anxiety is just supposed to be part of having a job. How can we possibly *not* worry, when shareholders want our reports or our boss reminds us every day they'll hold us accountable for every mistake we make?

Jesus wasn't telling us to deny trouble or to push it under the rug. It's smart to understand our situation and the options we have. He was simply reminding us that worry isn't a beneficial response to the challenges we have, particularly because only God knows the future that will unfold.

Worry stems from immersion in the fragility of the temporary world. It draws our attention away from God's eternal Kingdom, draining the strength we need to stay joyfully present for both personal and professional work.

Underneath Matthew 6:25-34 is a reminder of God's provision.[33] We often worry throughout our work that we must take care of everything ourselves and that there's no safety net. But Jesus says we don't have to worry specifically because He anchors our security, shouldering what scares us. He mercifully came into the world to ensure we didn't have to make atonement with our own sacrifice anymore. Through the compassionate power and omniscience of God, He knows what we need and never fails to show up.

Even in His mission, Jesus models how to hand God the worry that can break us.

As He prayed in the garden of Gethsemane, Jesus had every human reason to be afraid, knowing He would suffer and die on the cross. His worry was, by some scholars' interpretations, deep enough to bleed out of His skin (Luke 22:44). His voice likely wept with honesty as He said, "My Father, if it is possible, may this cup be taken from me" (Luke 22:42).

But in the same breath, He submitted to the will of God, understanding there is no worry or problem so large that God can't properly handle it.

It's OK to acknowledge when we're worried. But handing our worry to God in a Your-will-be-done faith is a profound act of worship that says, "I'm not big enough, but You are."

To think clearly, engage well, and persevere through even the hardest seasons, we have to give our worry to God—and trust that He will come through for us. Just as He was unlimited in His capacity to carry the burden of Jesus in the garden, He's unlimited in His capacity to shoulder what weighs us down, too.

Challenge

Identify one task, project, or situation at work that you've been worried about. List out what you would do if you were not worried about that issue. Perhaps that's approaching the project differently or sharing information with others.

Do at least one of the points you've put on your list. Whenever you feel yourself creeping back into worry-based thoughts, ask God to give you greater confidence in His provision. Remind yourself that, even though worry is normal, God's peace can exceed understanding (Philippians 4:6-7).

Reflection Questions

1. What are some of your most frequent or largest worries, in work or elsewhere?

2. What do you normally do when you are worried?

3. What did Jesus do when He was worried, such as in the garden of Gethsemane (Matthew 26:36-46)?

4. How would your life be different if you allowed God to remove the worries you have?

Week 31
Look for Little Miracles

Everyone was amazed and gave praise to God. They were filled
with awe and said, "We have seen remarkable things today."
—Luke 5:26

Just after Jesus called His first disciples, people lowered a paralyzed man down to Jesus from the roof of a building. So that the Pharisees would understand the authority and power He had on Earth, Jesus forgave the paralyzed man for his sins and restored his ability to walk.

The people around Him had their minds blown.

Sometimes, miracles happen in business, too.

The ornery client says yes.

The right supplier just "happens" to connect with the CEO.

Because those things are both surprising and delighting, we can be prompted to express gratitude to our team and to God.

But do you know what's also remarkable?

The new worker standing up against the pecking order of a business.

The manager sharing their lunch because a lower employee's reasonable wage isn't enough to handle their debt.

The CEO reaching out to someone in their network because a new employee needs a mentor.

We often overlook these small acts of kindness. They can get overshadowed by both the scandals on our social media feeds and the celebration around larger company goals. But they're the subtle earthquakes of God's ever-present love and help (Psalm 46:1),[34] evidence that He is working everywhere we are.

God doesn't shake us this way to break us. Rather, He does it to reveal where our instabilities are and to build us up stronger.

So many of us are giving everything we can and just need a little touch of grace to keep hope. In our weariness, we need to tremble together to reset and regain strength.

Look for little miracles. Be one, too.

Challenge

When you see a small evidence of God in your office or on your digital channels, be the lamp that shares the light (Matthew 5:16). Call attention to what you see and give praise so that others can better recognize how active and present God truly is. At the same time, commit to walking in humility, allowing your posture and character to point others toward the goodness of God.

Reflection Questions

1. How do you define "remarkable?"

2. What do you think might be keeping you from noticing more of the remarkable things around you?

3. What steps can you take to pay more attention to the remarkable things that are happening (or to show God a willingness to participate in them)?

4. Can you think of a time in your work or personal life when your success or broader journey seemed to have support from God?

Week 32
Take the Chance to Minister

Be very careful then, how you live—not as unwise but as wise,
making the most of every opportunity, because the days are evil.
—Ephesians 5:15-16

If everyone showed up to the company potluck in *Carpe Diem* t-shirts, nobody would blink—seizing fleeting opportunities is a core tenet of modern career culture.

The secular risk of not taking everyday opportunities is that we won't find the level of success we would if we put in real effort. But Ephesians 5:15-16 is not just about our own benefit. It's about thinking carefully about the chances we can take for God and—because we're surrounded by so much temptation and ungodly behavior—not wasting a single moment as one of His servants.

Everyday opportunities are less important than the opportunities we have to know God and Jesus. When we don't take those chances, we miss out on much of the joy He wants to share with us.

Even worse, we can do things that run contrary to what He wants and fail in the Great Commission to bring others to faith. When we connect the call for careful living to John 9:4 ("As long as it is day, we must do the works of him who sent me. Night is coming, when no one can work."), we get even greater understanding of how important it is to pay attention to what we're doing—we have a limited amount of time to give others the Good News so they might be saved.

In His wisdom, Jesus didn't always give everyone what they wanted (see Week 34). But He constantly responded to the chance to help in alignment with the glorification of God, even on his way to other places. Whether it was talking to Zaccheus in the tree or slowing down to make sure the woman with the hemorrhage understood she wouldn't bleed loneliness anymore, He *saw* people (Luke 5:25-34, 19:1-10).[35,36,37]

He sees us.

He sees you.

When we consider all the "great opportunities" that hit our email inbox or reveal themselves in yet another meeting, let's keep perspective: We don't have to say yes to everything. The real opportunities to prioritize are those in which we can learn about and minister for God.

Challenge

Based on the call in Ephesians 5:15-16, brainstorm how you can make each of your agenda points an opportunity to do good work for God: Can you connect others? Share uplifting feedback? Ask a blessing on the next meeting?

Alternatively, explore a new spiritual practice or space where God might be inviting you to grow, such as reading a new Christian book or attending a community event.

Whatever path you choose, ask God to help you notice the open doors around you—and to step through them with boldness.

Reflection Questions

1. Have you ever had opportunities you didn't take advantage of?

2. What areas of your life do you think Ephesians 5:15-16 most applies to?

3. What do you define as "unwise?" "Wise?"

4. What does God define as "unwise?" "Wise?"

Week 33
Take the Hard Feedback That Heals

Jesus answered them, "It is not the healthy who need a doctor, but the sick. I have not come to call the righteous, but sinners to repentance."—Luke 5:31-32

Professionals today are called to own our missteps—failing is how we grow.

Yet, most of us still hesitate to admit failure, not just because we're afraid of looking incompetent or being rejected, but also because there is a legitimate fear about keeping roles in an increasingly tight economy.

On one writing assignment, I severely miscalculated how long the draft would take to finish. Too embarrassed to admit I'd set an unrealistic deadline, I stayed up the entire night—not going to bed at all—to deliver.

The client was happy, but I was wrecked. I didn't have anyone who could come on short notice to watch my kids, and the day that followed was torturous. I vowed I would never sacrifice to that extreme for a client—or go that far to hide I'd been wrong—again.

Admitting sin is harder than admitting we turned in a report late or botched a supply order. That's because sins often come wrapped in false comfort. They give us something—a feeling of control, a momentary high—even as they pull us from God. Admitting sin means admitting we're lacking in a deeper way and trusting God to meet that need. It also means facing that we went against His will. If we're unsure about God's goodness, that honesty can feel terrifying.

Consider this workplace analogy as a complement to Jesus' metaphor in Luke 5:31-32: When someone is doing their job well, the boss doesn't interfere. But if the worker does poorly, the boss will give them more training or build an improvement plan.

In the same way, Jesus isn't looking for the people who have it all together. He's looking for the ones ready to admit they don't. He's ready to sit with us—like a good mentor with coffee and feedback—and offer a better way. But first, we have to ask for help, understanding that "God opposes the proud but shows favor to the humble" (James 4:6).

As we read Luke 5:31-32, ponder that *all* of us, as Christ-bearers, are called to serve as spiritual and physical doctors, as much as we are able, reflecting His drive for compassion. In picking up His cross, we pick up the responsibility to bear one another's burdens in intimate social care (Galatians 6:2).

In the 1998 film *Patch Adams* (based on a true story), medical student Hunter "Patch" Adams (Robin Williams) goes before the state medical board to defend himself against accusations of practicing medicine without a license. He asserts that every patient who came to his ranch is also a physician, with people being responsible for others even as they receive care. He questions the formality attached to the title of doctor and pleads for physicians to truly see people: "A doctor's mission should be not just to prevent death, but also *to improve the quality of life*. That's why you treat a disease, you win, you lose. *You treat a person, I guarantee you'll win*." [38]

The real-life Hunter Adams dedicated his life to reforming the Western approach to healthcare, believing that real connection and humor—pathways for God's joy—have the capacity for healing. [39] A host of studies now confirm the relationship between social connection and wellbeing, as noted by institutions such as the National Institutes of Health, World Health Organization, and the Centers for Disease Control and Prevention. [40,41,42]

Just as Adams paid it forward to his patients, and just as the disciples paid it forward after learning from Jesus, we can heal and be healed.

Where do you need Jesus to coach you, and who could you see better?

Challenge

It's easy to stay stuck in habits or cycles that don't honor God when we don't take time to dig into the Word or pray. Culture can play a big role here, with work and other responsibilities distracting us away from the Lord.

To help people overcome this hurdle so they can learn and repent, identify some individuals in your workplace who might need spiritual support. Take something off their plate so they have space to seek what God says and Who He is. Try to get to know them, because *people often need to use the trust they have with other people as a steppingstone to learning to trust God*. In helping them embrace Him and His irrevocable truth, we "save them from death and cover a multitude of sins" (James 5:19-20).

Reflection Questions

1. Have you had a time in your life when you felt spiritually unwell? If so, what was happening?

2. What are some ways people can be spiritually sick?

3. What has helped restore your spiritual health in the past?

4. In what ways might you bring others to spiritual or physical wellness using the gifts God has provided to you?

Week 34
Ask with Reverent Confidence

In the morning, Lord, you hear my voice; in the morning I lay my requests before you and wait expectantly. —Psalm 5:3

As professionals, we're constantly sending out emails or applications—and then waiting in expectation—so that we can move forward.

The hope is that the news we receive back will be good. But in the risk management part of our brain, we know we might wait only to hear nothing.

God can say no to us when we make a request, too.

This doesn't seem to jive well with what Jesus tells us in Matthew 7:7. Aren't we supposed to be able to ask for anything—money, a house, the best corner office—and have God give it? Isn't God supposed to open the door any time we knock? If we believe it, we'll receive it—that's the heart of prosperity gospel preaching.[43]

To understand the limitations of this verse, we have to kneel with Jesus in the garden of Gethsemane (Mark 14:32-42). In His most desperate hour, Jesus poured out His agony to God, acknowledging the power of the Almighty as He asked the Father to take His cup from Him.

But Jesus immediately then accepted the will of God (see Week 30).

We often assume, simply because of fickle feelings like excitement or fear, that our requests and the will of God are synonymous. They often aren't.

The Lord can be direct with us about His plans when He needs to be, such as when He told Joshua to take Jericho (Joshua 6). But because God, acknowledging the limitations in our understanding and discernment, does not reveal all His mysteries to us, we can't claim to know every facet of what His will is.

God is not a vending machine.[44] He's smart and loving enough to turn down most of what we ask for because He knows better. As

Robin Jones Gunn puts it, "If God gave us everything we asked for, we'd be in chaos."

God also is under no obligation to grant us whatever we please. He is not and never has been in debt to us—in fact, the point of Jesus dying on the cross was to pay the sin debt we owe God that we cannot possibly reconcile on our own.

Why, then, did Jesus teach we could ask for anything?

Jesus was speaking to people who understood what it was like to have a barrier between them and God. They had to approach Him with caution and sacrifice. It would have been hard for them to imagine a kind of intimacy with Him where they could make any request without fear or protocol. Jesus was trying to reframe their image of God's character to help them understand the kind of loving relationship He was about to redeem for them.

John emphasized this idea of coming to God in boldness when we consider Him first: "This is the confidence we have in approaching God: that if we ask anything according to his will, he hears us. And if we know that he hears us—whatever we ask—we know that we have what we asked of him" (1 John 5:14-15).

When we make a request with respect for God's sovereignty, we never have to question His ability to meet the need behind it. He's never going to run into supply chain issues. His single leaders can defeat hundreds (1 Kings 18:20–40), and His teams can win even when outnumbered by thousands (Judges 7).

That's why our requests should land first on God's desk. He has the power to make anything succeed—and the wisdom to grant what will truly bless. When King Solomon asked for wisdom, God honored the request because King Solomon had humbled himself for the glory of God and Israel. James 1:5 assures us that God is still that generous today—when we ask in faith for what reflects His will, He will not withhold it.

We shouldn't dare to approach God as though He *must* say yes. But neither should we approach Him in vain. Because of Who He is, our expectation is not foolish—it's faithful.

Challenge

As we make requests of God, it's easy to let our egos take over. To help center your heart, focus on the fact that He already knows your needs and wants to shape your desires through a relationship with Him.

Within the limitations of what God allows us to know, try including at least one request that prioritizes God and aligns with His character—e.g., "Lord, would you give me the courage to preach to somebody about You today?" Asking for what honors Him helps put our personal requests into better perspective.

Reflection Questions

1. What would you ask God for if you had no doubts or anxieties?

2. In what ways does your request reflect your desire to honor God?

3. Are there any things you shouldn't request from God? If so, what and why?

4. How might your life change if you started each day with a prayer that reflected both your needs and your desire to serve God?

Week 35
Seek the Fruit Before the Metrics

But the fruit of the Spirit is love, joy, peace, forbearance, kindness, goodness, faithfulness, gentleness and self-control. Against such things there is no law.—Galatians 5:22-23

For a company, good fruit means increased assets, an improved or steadfast reputation, or expansion. For a worker, good fruit means productivity, strong interpersonal relationships with team members, opportunities, and advancement. All these are quantifiable. For example, we might give our supervisor a satisfaction rating.

We usually take the lack of visible fruit as a sign that there is a deficiency that needs remedying. We try to transform the company or train workers to fill perceived gaps. Individuals who fail to produce good fruit even after transformation or training attempts can be quickly replaced with people who might be more able to succeed.

Because of this underlying emphasis on quantifiable positives, the non-quantifiable fruit of the Spirit that Paul listed can get lost in the shuffle. It becomes easier for us to focus on whether the business or person looks good on paper, with everything becoming about meeting quotas and "worthy" objective key results (OKRs).

Imagine what would happen if we approached Jesus this way.

"How many people did you heal his quarter?"

"How quickly can you get those fish and bread delivered—we've got 5,000 customers waiting!"

"Lazarus' family just gave a low satisfaction score. How can we improve your delivery speed for next time?"

God can beat every quantification tool we've got, precisely reporting even the number of hairs on our head from His core (Matthew 10:29-31). But *Jesus didn't die to satisfy a metric—He died to ensure that every person He counts as faithful will always have access to the fruit of the Spirit in a quality relationship with God.*

When a business operates under Christian principles, the fruit of the Spirit is given just as much weight—if not more—than the quantifiable measures of success and, in fact, is used as a foundation to get what is measurable. The fruit of the Spirit always serves as a component of healthy workplace culture and psychological safety.

Just like improving skills might mean going to a mentor, improving the fruit of the Spirit means going to and spending time with God. It requires trusting in Who He is and modeling His character in our thoughts, behaviors, and vision (see Week 20). The more intimate we are with the Father, the more He will use us as conduits for the Spirit's good things.

Challenge

It's not unusual for people to be unaware of how their spiritual gifts manifest the fruit of the Spirit—we don't always recognize the specific ways God has equipped us. You might not be aware that you have a gift for creating policy (administration), offering good insights (wisdom), or uplifting others (exhortation). This lack of awareness can come from poor feedback, environmental and resource limitations, cognitive distortions, or even a deliberate choice to avoid self- or relational awareness.

To correct this issue, try asking others what they perceive your spiritual gifts to be. Alternatively, take a spiritual gifts inventory online. Use your results to inform your decisions about what to pursue in your work relationships and how to contribute. To have even greater influence, join forces with someone who has a complementary gift.

Reflection Questions

1. Where do you most clearly see the fruit of the Spirit in your workplace? Where does it seem most absent?

2. How could you demonstrate the fruit of the Spirit going forward?

3. How is each fruit of the Spirit different and important?

4. What fruit of the Spirit sparks the biggest positive response in you? What feels more distant or less energizing? Why?

Week 36

Safeguard Your Body as Sacred

Do you not know that your bodies are temples of the Holy Spirit, who is in you, whom you have received from God? You are not your own; you were bought at a price. Therefore honor God with your bodies. —1 Corinthians 6:19-20

In 2017, Japanese media worker Miwa Sado made headlines after dying from heart failure. In the month prior to her death, she had taken only two days off and worked 159 hours of overtime. Officials ruled her passing as karoshi, or death by overwork.[45]

Overwork is well-known in Asian countries, but it's a global issue—the World Health Organization (WHO) and International Labour Organization reported in 2021 that there were 745,194 deaths attributable to long work hours.[46] The rate of overwork-related death connected to stroke and heart disease increased 29 percent from 2000 to 2016.[47] As technology continues to blur home-work boundaries, it's only getting easier to clock more hours.

Professionals are using science to push back more strongly against unreasonable work demands. We know, for example, that rest allows the creative parts of the brain to become more active, thereby supporting problem solving and innovation.[48]

But this view is purely pragmatic: Put rest in, get creativity, product, or service out.

1 Corinthians 6:19-20, which warns against sexual immorality, helps us start to see that the way we treat our bodies has both physical and moral ramifications. In the office, we might abuse our authority to coerce subordinates into intimacy or cover up acts of sexual violence. We sometimes get caught up in passionate, reciprocal temptation, too—it's tough to hold physical boundaries when mutual attraction is clear and we're together in the same space for so much of the day! Either way, the emotional and spiritual fallout can be devastating.

That we're called to protect our bodies in everyday ways—for example, eating well, delegating as Moses did to be able to rest (Exodus 18), or refusing to lean on caffeine or Adderall—is implied in the way Scripture describes them as temples of the Holy Spirit.

There's respect for God in it when we ask after our own wellbeing: *Do I truly feel ready to tackle the day for the Lord in the morning? Or do I push myself based on a sense of shame and potential loss?*

We can't anticipate every variable that could reduce our safety. But we can try to be intentional about putting some safeguards in place that treat the body as sacred rather than expendable, such as finding a workout buddy or dressing modestly. If you need motivation for that, consider how Jesus allowed His body to be broken to protect yours.

Challenge

Find at least one area of self-care you could improve, such as getting more sleep or improving your diet. Then look at your company policies. Are they contributing to physical self-neglect or risk in any way? A policy that allows inconsistent shift scheduling, for instance, might make it easier to dismiss your body's normal cues for rest.

If there isn't already a policy that supports healthier physical rhythms or safeguards your wellbeing, work with the appropriate channels—such as Human Resources—to advocate for a realistic one. Consult local, state, and federal regulations in developing or proposing any changes.

Reflection Questions

1. How does seeing your body as a temple connect to doing good work for God?

2. In what ways do you misuse your body? Protect it?

3. What do you think you could accomplish for yourself or God if your body were always well taken care of and protected?

4. What steps can you take—personally or professionally—to change physical habits or environments that aren't honoring your body as God's temple?

Week 37
Follow Through, Finish Strong

...being confident in this, that he who began a good work in you
will carry it on to completion until the day of Christ Jesus.
—Philippians 1:6

Is there somebody on your team who has fantastic skills but can't seem to finish much of what they start?

Maybe they break out of the gate strong, full of energy and inspiration. But soon, their motivation deflates like a sad balloon.

Maybe the can't-get-it-done member of the team is you.

I let one novella languish on a shelf for *15 years*. I got trapped in the feeling that the entire story concept wasn't good enough. But I couldn't throw it away, either.

Then, after a conversation with my daughter sparked a moment of clarity, I wrote the second half. The final draft—a Victorian-esque slapstick that uses a baby alien's adventure to explore the deepest, most universal elements of humanity—helped me feel comfortable expanding my range. What once felt like a dead-end became one of my favorite pieces.

For me, the biggest overall hurdle to follow-through has been a lack of money and mentors. But there are lots of reasons we fizzle: We get distracted by other interests, overwhelmed by the sheer scope of the work, or paralyzed by our inner critic.

Thankfully, we have a God Who models perseverance better than anyone.

God doesn't just start things. He finishes them with eternal, covenantal faithfulness, knowing from the beginning how Jesus factors into our story: "And I will put enmity between you and the woman, and between your offspring and hers; he will crush your head, and you will strike his heel" (Genesis 3:15).

There's no project He's more committed to than you.[49]

God's not giving up on you. He's sharpening you through service, deepening your insight through revelation, and working in you until Jesus comes to bring it all to completion.

If you struggle with follow-through, take heart: God hasn't lost sight of the finish line. Let His commitment to you fuel your commitment to what matters. Then ask Him what projects He's asking you to persevere with—and which ones He's asking you to release.

Challenge

Identify one priority project from the ones you haven't finished. Outline specific action steps to move the project forward, recognizing that your willingness to act is part of how God shapes your follow-through.

If you want extra encouragement to finish your work, ask someone to hold you accountable for the steps you choose.

Reflection Questions

1. What kind of "good work" do you think Paul meant in Philippians 1:6? How might that relate to your own projects or growth?

2. How can you show others that God is working in you?

3. What part of the "good work" do you think is done in you? What part is yet to be finished?

4. How do you think you will change as God moves you to completion?

Week 38
Invite God into Your Joy

...I will celebrate before the Lord.—2 Samuel 6:21

Maybe it's happened to you—you work ridiculously hard to get a win for your company, working overtime and making sacrifices. Then, when the win comes and the party happens, nobody even mentions your name. No "Thank you!" or pat on the back. Just silence, like you're invisible.

We don't just overlook *people* when the champagne pops. We overlook God, too.

God's on our team. He doesn't sit on the bench, but rather leads the front line day and night (Exodus 13:21), controlling whether we fail or are victorious.

He likes parties, too—He's got a massive one planned for our homecoming (Luke 15:11-31), and Jesus likely wasn't sitting in the corner like a grumpy grandpa at the wedding at Cana (John 2:1-12).[50,51]

So, why do we so often fail to include Him with gratitude and joy in our celebrations?

Part of the problem might be the trouble we have balancing God's relatability and intimacy—embodied in Jesus—with His holy sovereignty.[52] It's hard to relax and bust a move when we know the Guest next to us could take out the universe with a simple wink.

But the corporate world also sends a strong message that success is due to individual effort and accountability, rather than blessing. Humbling ourselves to celebrate in a way that recognizes how much God contributes runs contrary to this narrative and sparks a fear of potential conflict (see Weeks 2 and 46).

But it respects Him in a way He can honor.

Including God in our festivities starts with slowing down. Celebration is meant to include the full expression of emotion, as well as reflection. From both the biological and psychological perspectives, this process takes time. All too often, however, instead of giving each other the proper time we need to internalize and be empowered by the wins that happen through God, we pressure each other to move rapidly to The Next Important Thing.

Instead of rushing to the next task, pause. Give yourself—and others—the space to reflect on how He's been moving (see Week 21). When we honor and delight in Him like this, He's not just in the party room—He's at the center, leading the dance.

Challenge

Look for opportunities throughout your workday to celebrate with God. Perhaps that means taking five minutes to dance to a worship song. Maybe it means taking a minute to tell God thanks. Maybe you buy yourself the bigger coffee from the cafeteria and mentally share it with Him.[53]

However you celebrate with Him, stay fully present in the joy. Whatever needs to happen in five minutes can wait.

Reflection Questions

1. What ways of celebrating with God feel most natural for you? Least?

2. Do you find it easy to celebrate with God overall? Why or why not?

3. What does your ideal celebration look like?

4. Why is it important to celebrate with God?

Week 39

Check the Impact Before You Act

Therefore, as we have opportunity, let us do good to all people,
especially to those who belong to the family of believers.
—Galatians 6:10

Would you trust a driver who couldn't see the road or follow their GPS map?

We have confidence when a leader can see where to go. That's why we go to such pains to create vision statements—they answer the question, "Why are we doing this work?" and reveal what the company wants to be or manifest.

For most teams, the company vision attaches to some specific, foundational value or belief, such as "Keeping the planet healthy is important." Once we identify our core belief, we target it in a specific way by developing specific products or services. This unique "how" becomes our mission statement.

But what happens if we think something is good and it isn't?

Take the iPhone. Lauded as one of the biggest innovations in history, the latest iterations allow us to listen to music, watch videos, participate in a meeting, send an email, or even compare prices on something we want to buy.

Yet, many sociologists and educators assert that the invention of the smartphone has created serious social problems, such as reduced inability to focus and increased depression.

It's a sobering reminder that even the most celebrated ideas can have unintended consequences if we don't check our direction against lasting values.

Because we're created in Jesus for good works (Ephesians 2:10), we're obligated to slow down and think about the full potential influence of what we put into the world. Once we know our solutions won't bring unintended harm, we can let our actions prove we're committed to our vision. In this way, we can let our light shine before others, serving as an example (Matthew 5:14-16).

Work culture, however, can make slowing down and verifying our positive influence difficult. Protocols and scripts can make it harder to connect and communicate, or the pressure to increase profit margins might make us afraid to challenge a bad policy that hurts employees, customers, or the environment.

This is where courage and perseverance have their place. They allow us to challenge the too-fast status quo, lobby for what's right, and protect everything that sits inside the positive vision we create.

You might have to circle the Jericho—e.g., extreme competitiveness, a lack of resources, resistance to change—that impedes your good for many days before the walls finally crumble (Joshua 6). But just as God was with Joshua, He's also with you. The resistance you might face with a God-given vision might be fierce, but sacred ground always comes with sacred backing.

Don't give up. Walk around the city one more time.[54]

Challenge

Find one area of work where you've been slacking in taking opportunities to do good, such as participating in volunteer projects or helping to keep a common area of the office organized and clean. Seize some of those opportunities!

Once you've taken personal steps, look outward: How might workplace policies, procedures, and norms be adjusted to support a culture of greater interpersonal provision, care, protection, and service (see Week 32)?

Lastly, explore inversion thinking.[55] This is a problem-solving method that starts by imagining failure or harm, works backward to identify where the breakdowns would occur, and then develops proactive solutions to prevent the damage. Using this technique can mitigate some of the risks that could derail the positive work you'd like to do.

Reflection Questions

1. What types of good are easy for you to do? Difficult?

2. Which types of people or groups do you find it easiest or hardest to do good for?

3. How might you create more opportunities for others to do good?

4. How might you stay resolved to do good even if others criticize or doubt you for it?

Week 40
Handle What You Have with Wisdom

We want to avoid any criticism of the way we administer this liberal gift. For we are taking pains to do what is right, not only in the eyes of the Lord but also in the eyes of man.
—2 Corinthians 8:20-21

When the apostle Paul wrote his second letter to the Corinthians, he urged them to follow through on collecting money for believers in Jerusalem who were suffering. Holding to this promise was necessary to show others there was nothing to fault in their faith, model the grace and power of Jesus, and attract more believers.

Just like the early Christians, we observe how leaders handle the money they have. Many leaders fail to do what is right by committing embezzlement, giving themselves exorbitant salaries, or channeling funds to specific causes or projects that customers and employees are not aligned with. When offenses are deliberately committed like this, they erode the trust and reputation of the business quickly.

But sometimes, companies are like the wicked servant in Jesus' parable of the talents (Matthew 25:13-40). They might not intend to do wrong with the money, but they don't manage it in a productive way that benefits anyone, which defeats the purpose of the investment.

Any time money comes into our accounts, we're wise to ask if we're maximizing the potential within those funds.

Will others who audit our financial decisions feel that they have been informed and trusted through our decision-making process?

What messages have we sent through the way we have allocated and communicated about our funds?

The more transparent, cooperative, and effective we are with our assets, the less likely it is that we'll experience the type of public criticism Paul wanted to avoid, and the more likely it is that we'll find the approval enjoyed by the first servant in Jesus' parable.

Challenge

Take time this week to evaluate what's been entrusted to you in your work—whether it's finances, data, equipment, time, or people. Seek feedback from managers, mentors, or trusted colleagues to gain perspective on how you're stewarding these responsibilities. Supplement their input with research as needed. This might include industry standards, social listening, or performance data.

But remember: Even advice that's widely accepted can fall short if it contradicts God's truth. Because public trends don't always align with God's will, invite the Holy Spirit to guide you with discernment through regular prayer.

Reflection Questions

1. What money, property, or responsibilities are you currently stewarding? Seeing healthy ambition in Luke 16:10, is there something you wish you could oversee? If so, why?

2. What are the practical and spiritual consequences of administering well? Poorly?

3. Have you ever witnessed or heard of a time when resources were mishandled? What impression did that leave on you?

4. Can you define "doing what is right, not only in the eyes of the Lord but also in the eyes of man?"

Week 41
Credit God for All Success

You may say to yourself, "My power and the strength of my hands have produced this wealth for me." But remember the Lord your God, for it is he who gives you the ability to produce wealth, and so confirms his covenant, which he swore to your forefathers, as it is today.—Deuteronomy 8:17-18

There's no shortage of people on social media who readily take credit for everything they achieve. Some do this with graciousness. Less humble folks blatantly show off what they've earned, posting about "living their best life" through their newest car, home, vacation, or other purchases. Their favorite words are "I did it!" Particularly in American culture, those words are hallowed as echoes of grit and capitalistic entrepreneurism.

But as Proverbs 16:18 reminds us, "Pride goes before destruction, a haughty spirit before a fall."

Jesus showed us the opposite path. Even as He asserted He had all authority, He acknowledged that that authority—and everything He accomplished with it—was possible through God (Matthew 28:18).

Make no mistake: God delivers people into our paths with intention, and every gift and ability is God-given, which we see in Exodus 31. And although the craftsmen of Moses' time were tasked to build a physical tabernacle, today Christians are charged with using their talents to build the church. When we get lost in pride and believe that our success comes only from ourselves, it is easy to lose sight of that mission, forget to testify about the enormous role God has in our wins (see Week 38), and give Him the gratitude He deserves (see Week 3).

We can acknowledge the effort we put in using what God gave us. It's healthy to know what we've tapped to succeed and to admit the size of the mountains we've overcome. But as corporate leaders encourage a team mentality and the use of "we" instead of "I," let's put a spiritual spin on the cue. Let's recognize our partnership with

God, put proper credit where it's due, and stop pretending we alone call the shots.

Challenge

Identify at least one win you've had this week, even if it's as simple as finally cleaning off your desk. Reflect on the abilities God gave you that helped make it happen. Thank Him for each one.

If you've achieved a larger breakthrough, such as a promotion or closing an important deal, break down the steps that led to that moment. Be specific about the skills involved and give thanks that God orchestrated each part of the sequence.

Looking ahead, try to shift your internal narrative. Instead of saying "I did that," say, "Thank you, God, for doing that through me!" It's a simple way to acknowledge His ongoing role in your journey.

Reflection Questions

1. How might you encourage someone else to recognize God's role in their successes?

2. If God provides the ability to produce wealth, how should you see your work?

3. Why is it important to God that He deliver wealth and other good things to you, as indicated by Deuteronomy 8:17-18?

4. What safeguard habits might you develop to stay more mindful of God's role in your success (see Week 5)?

Week 42
Persist When Others Don't Get It

Moses thought that his own people would realize that God was using him to rescue them, but they did not. —Acts 7:25

Maybe you've been there. You do everything you can to deliver your important data or message well. But instead of being grateful, the people you're trying to reach throw rotten tomatoes at you. They shoot down what you've said, roll their eyes, or even tell you to get lost.

Entrepreneurs and executives often face this scenario as they try to persuade others their idea has value. Their rejection is no small source of self-doubt and pain, especially when experts within an industry—who are supposed to be most likely to understand—are the ones doing the rejecting.

But imagine if you were responsible for the moral wellbeing of an entire people, not just marketing an innovative product. From this perspective, Moses carried a far heavier burden, understanding that the affliction of his fellow Hebrews would continue until they finally accepted that he wasn't bonkers and was, in fact, a servant of the Lord.

Later, Jesus picked up the burden of Moses. "He came to that which was his own, but his own did not receive him" (John 1:11).

As Christian professionals, we'll have moments when, like Moses and Jesus, we're mocked when we try to help or innovate. We'll have periods when, again and again, we have to pray in loving intercession on behalf of other people as they complain about us and our alleged incompetence.

But ultimately, with God's help, Moses and Jesus both got the job done. They didn't quit, even when others didn't grasp their mission or authority.

In the same way, when we feel called to a mission, let's not allow others to determine whether we stop or advance. Let's listen only to

159

God, trusting that He will permit the mission to succeed through us. Just as Moses did when Israel complained, we can remind Him when we feel like the burden is too heavy to carry alone (Numbers 11:10-17; Exodus 5:22-6:13). As God did with Moses, He will deliver others—people like Jethro, Aaron, Hur, and the judges—who can help us, according to the size of the burden entrusted.

Challenge

When you encounter people who don't understand how God is using you, resist the urge to judge them harshly for their lack of understanding. Instead, be compassionate, imitating how Jesus asked God to forgive those who crucified Him because they didn't know what they were doing (Luke 23:24).

Ask yourself why they might be blind to your purpose or desire to help. What biases or information gaps might be getting in the way? How can you eliminate those biases and gaps?

Ask yourself and God how you can continue forward with conviction—full face to the wind—even when others doubt your calling.

Reflection Questions

1. Why do you think the people of Israel failed to see or appreciate what Moses was trying to do?

2. In Acts 7, what was Stephen's purpose in reminding the people how Israel had resisted Moses?

3. Think about a time when others didn't listen to you as you tried to do something good. How did it feel? What did you learn?

4. What interpersonal strategies can you use to deal with people who don't see your purpose or good intentions—as in the examples of Moses or Stephen?

Week 43
Give God Even Your Gripes

Therefore I will not keep silent; I will speak out in the anguish of my spirit, I will complain in the bitterness of my soul. —Job 7:11

We all know Debbie. Whining and complaining, she's a bit of a downer.

Nobody likes Debbie.

Or at least, that's what often goes through our heads when we feel like griping. We think that if we open our mouths to talk about what's bothering us, others will ream us for it in one way or another. The blanket of toxic positivity so often present in corporate offices convinces us it's better to stay silent because *maybe we're just not trying hard enough* or *it's not all that bad* (see Week 4).

But quite often, like Job, we have legitimate reasons to gripe—a crappy boss, being cheated in return for hard work, or getting lost in red tape.

In those moments, you're not Debbie Downer if you go to God and tell Him the truth about how you feel. You're one of His kids who is genuinely unhappy and who needs someone to understand that you're suffering unfairly.

God greatly desires your gripes, because in them you are honest and show faith that He will hear you out.

Spew everything. He can handle it.

The only thing you can't do? Blame God for your woe and curse Him. Job's own wife told him to do this (Job 2:9). But Job knew two things: He knew he had not sinned, and he knew his place against the Creator he trusted to do the right thing.

And remember: It was not God who destroyed everything Job had. It was the Devil. It gave God great pain to see His servant suffer. He took no pleasure in it and stayed with Job through everything. But God allowed the Devil to destroy Job's assets and loved ones to put the Devil in his place and prove that God's assessment of Job as loyal and righteous was the correct one. Without that rebuke, without *teaching the Devil* that Job would, in fact, hold the line, the Devil would have gained ground.

Later, Jesus would suffer and cry out to God—"My God, my God, why have you forsaken me?" (Matthew 27:46)—despite having not sinned, too, and for the same reason.

If you must gripe, gripe. God wants to know you even when you feel bleh or want to punch things. He will listen, and so long as your faith is in Him, He will never work against you.

Challenge

When you feel like lamenting to God, try to remove any filters that make you hold back your real thoughts and worries. After all, God already knows what's in your heart. Give Him full authenticity. Lay out exactly what you are struggling with and ask Him to show you a path forward.

This kind of deep disclosure might feel awkward or difficult—culture often enforces boundaries around confession. But keep practicing. The more you experience God's gentleness in response to your honesty, the easier being open with God will become.

Reflection Questions

1. What anguishes have you felt comfortable confessing to God? Which ones have felt harder to bring to Him?

2. What was Job's true anguish (Job 7:20, 27:6)?

3. How do you typically complain—aloud, internally, or through others? How does that compare to how Job lamented?

4. When you bring your complaints to God, what kind of response do you hope for? Why?

Week 44
Hold Everything with an Open Hand

For this world in its present form is passing away.
—1 Corinthians 7:31

One of the biggest dangers that comes with corporate life is that, even with all our talk of adapting to change, we quickly settle into the way things are—our commute, office culture, or even how many pages we print each week. This kind of routine can cause a negative mental fixedness that halts innovation in its tracks. Spiritually, we can start imagining that payscales and org charts are permanent fixtures that will matter when Jesus comes back.

(Spoiler: They aren't, and they won't.)

Jesus was clear that those who were used to being first on Earth will get an awakening when He comes back (Matthew 23:11-12). And in Ecclesiastes 3-5, King Solomon cautions us that nothing we labor for will come with us into the next life.

I've had to reckon with this hard in my writing pursuits. Multiple agents told me my pitches and concepts were excellent. They *also* politely refused to represent me—unless I had at least 5,000-10,000 social media followers (I didn't), they couldn't sell my nonfiction books to large, traditional publishers, who would see that following as a safer bet for book sales and ROI. At the same time, I learned how some writers **manipulate bestseller lists** using techniques such as purchasing their own books.[56]

Rather than give up, I saved my pennies and self-published. But it forced me to abandon my original intended path, acknowledge that not everyone at the top of my industry gets there by skill, and concede that merit, effort, and talent aren't always what opens doors.

Whether we're flush with cash, climbing the ladder, or serving hundreds of clients, we must hold it all with an open hand and be willing to take an unplanned path—or even completely let go (see Week 24). Nothing compares to what God offers in eternity.

Hold loosely to what you've built, being willing to pivot, release goals you've idolized, or relinquish what you've acquired, as God tells you through prayer, Scripture, or wise counsel from others. Let Him shape your ambition toward His glory, because He's coming—in His time—with something better.

Challenge

Buy some inexpensive modeling clay or Play-Doh. Shape the dough into any figure you like. Place the Play-Doh in an airtight bag or container so it won't dry out. The next day, squash the figure and make a new one. Repeat for each day of the week.

As you shape and reshape the clay or Play-Doh, think about how God shapes your life in unexpected ways. Each time you reshape the clay, remind yourself of the freedom that comes from letting go of what's familiar. Jesus calls us to stay ready, even when we don't know the hour He may come (Matthew 25:1–13).

Take comfort in knowing that God is always willing to reshape you—not once, but every day—into someone more faithful, rooted in Him, and aligned with His purpose.

Reflection Questions

1. When the world as we know it passes away, what will remain?

2. If Ecclesiastes 3:9–14 teaches that enjoying work is a gift from God even though the world will pass away, how does John 9:4 call us to reciprocate the gift with diligence—using our work purposefully toward His mission?

3. What part of the world would you most want God to keep or eliminate? Why?

4. If you knew the world would pass away tomorrow, what would you do differently today? What keeps you from that path?

Week 45
Discover Your Gifted Authority

When Jesus had finished saying these things, the crowds were amazed at his teaching, because he taught as one having authority, and not as their teachers of the law.—Matthew 7:28-29

For many of us who worked our way up, the idea of gifted authority is appalling. It can conjure up bad memories of leaders whose family members took over and did a horrible job, having neither the desire nor skill to sit at the top. History is full of such transitions, both in politics and business.

But Jesus didn't sit in the temple teaching at just twelve years old because of nepotism (Luke 2:41-52). God granted Jesus the authority to speak because Jesus already carried the heart and mind of His Father. He knew Who He was, believed in His mission, and taught from intimate knowledge of God. God trusted Him because of those things.

I've been asked to write on behalf of CEOs and public leaders—people who shape organizations and influence policy. When I got those first contracts, I questioned my own credibility: "I'm a freelancer, not an executive. I don't have their experience, certifications, or titles. Who am I to speak in their voice?"

But I discovered that my authority rested in a unique ability to understand, clarify, and magnify the truth of their distinct stories and voices. I didn't need to be *like them* because my ability to listen underneath the surface for the heart of their insights was its own God-given gift.

Do you know who you really are? Do you believe in what you're doing and the values behind it? Do you understand those you represent so well that you have an innate sense of the words and tactics they would use and why they matter? Have you developed the skills the job takes?

When you can say yes to those questions, you'll carry your own quiet authority—not from pride, but from clarity. You'll know why you are in the room and trust your ability to speak.

Get solid about yourself, your cause, your gifts, and the One who sent you. It will completely change the way you open your mouth.

Challenge

When you need to speak with authority, don't let your mind balloon the stakes or expectations. Remember that you're only delivering a message with a small scope for the immediate moment, not delivering a massive address to set up 100 or 1,000 moments in the future.

Ask yourself how you feel. Based on your needs, personality, and preferences, what tactics could help you feel calmer and more confident?

Start with simple techniques, such as grounding your feet on the floor. Then apply deeper strategies, such as radical willingness, where you embrace your nerves or fear and remind yourself it's OK to feel every emotion.

You don't need to silence your nerves to speak with strength. Simply have courage—the ability, by definition, to do something even in the face of fear, pain, or grief.

Reflection Questions

1. What can you do to address people who might not want you to speak with authority in your profession or about God?

2. What most often keeps you from speaking with authority?

3. What level of authority are you most comfortable with? Does that match the goals you have for your career?

4. In what ways can a team or organization develop the same good authority as an individual?

Week 46
Drop the Mask, Let God Be Captain

Many are the plans in a person's heart, but it is the Lord's purpose that prevails. —Proverbs 19:21

Plans are to the business world what peanut butter and jelly are to sandwiches. Sure, they can be messy to put together, but they feel reliable and tend to please the crowd.

They're also one of the biggest masks we have against our lack of control (see Week 2).

Plans help workers at all levels feel secure. But we're human. Even good plans we make can have flaws that competitors can exploit.

More importantly, God—Whose understanding far exceeds ours—can easily disrupt any plan we design. In this sense, *the biggest mistake we tend to make as professionals is substituting sincere trust in God with our own strategies and tactics.*

We often plow forward believing in our own sequences and concepts, assuming we are the captain of our own ship. Perhaps this is because the world says business requires rationality, autonomy, and experience. Faith does not, by comparison, seem to hold those things.

Consider the story of Lazarus in John 11. Mary and Martha's plan for helping and avoiding sorrow was straightforward: Have Jesus come and heal their brother. But that plan didn't align with God's. Jesus intentionally delayed His arrival so that He could raise Lazarus, demonstrate the authority given to Him by God, and foreshadow His own escape from the tomb (see Week 34).

Because God's plans must always cover ours, bring to mind first the words of Jeremiah 29:11 in which God reassures us that He knows the plans He has for us, and that He wants to prosper us. In the context of Israel's exile in Babylon, those words are not a reassurance we will be able to escape immediate hardships, nor are they a guarantee we'll get whatever material gains we want. Rather, they convey that *God is with us even through suffering*, and that His big-picture, long-term intent for those who place faith in Him is loving (see Weeks 2 and 4).

Secondly, stay flexible in humility. When we surrender to God and remain willing to pivot in whatever direction He guides us, success has perfect odds.

Challenge

Make a list of all the plans you had through the week that didn't pan out. Include even simple things, such as not being able to enjoy your morning coffee because your toddler woke up earlier than usual. Use the list to gain perspective on how little control we truly have.

Reflect on how some inconveniences or disappointments end up being blessings in disguise. For example, some people had tickets to board the Titanic but, for one reason or another, didn't get on the ship. Their changed plans saved their lives. Identify at least one case from your own life where, in hindsight, you can see God's loving intervention.

If you are in the middle of a disruption now, ask how God might be directing you to something better and more meaningful.

Reflection Questions

1. When things don't go as planned, how do you usually react?

2. What kind of things do you like (or hate) to plan for? Why?

3. Starting with the story of creation and going all the way to Jesus' death, what does Scripture show us about God's ability to build and implement plans (see Week 11)?

4. How might you resist the temptation to try to take the helm away from God?

Week 47
Make God Your True Passion

Blessed is the one who does not walk in step with the wicked or stand in the way that sinners take or sit in the company of mockers, but whose delight is in the law of the Lord, and who meditates on his law day and night.—Psalm 1:1-2

A common mantra in business is to follow your passion. Love music? Do the work to be the next Taylor Swift or *The Beatles*. Enjoy being scrappy? Learn how to turn failing companies around with the assets they've got.

But what if your delight was on the Word and rules of God?

What if you put as much thought and energy into following Him as the math whiz gives to their formulas or the singer gives to their songs?

What would be different?

Psalm 1:1-2 isn't saying we must be reading Scripture and praying 24/7. Logistically and physically, that's just not going to happen. Rather, it's saying that, when we have mature faith, God and what He says will be the priority. Our thoughts will constantly come back to Him, no matter the time on the clock, because our heart is on His schedule and desiring Him as much as He desires us.

It's worth noting that passion in this context is not just strong enjoyment or interest. The root word of *passion* is the Latin verb *pati*, which means to suffer or endure. *When you're passionate about God, you delight in Him so much that you are willing to withstand difficulty and pain for Him, just as Jesus delights in you so much that He was willing to withstand difficulty and pain for you on the cross* (2 Samuel 22:20).

For a lot of us, this is a tough pill to swallow. There are just too many tasks, fires to put out, and other responsibilities to handle. How can we delight in and be passionate about God when so many other demands are on our plate? Surely, He must understand how many emails are jamming our inboxes!

But we are to have no other gods or idols, and *that includes work.*

What have you been loving? Is God at the top of your list? Or has He gotten shoved into the back closet along with the janitor's broom?

If you aren't able to consider Him and the Word well, it's not too late to change your roles and responsibilities.

Challenge

Download a Bible app to stay in the Word throughout your day. Each time you face an interaction or decision, pause to ask, "What does the Bible say about this?" Be ravenously curious and seek out scriptural stories or connections you haven't seen, rather than leaning on the most popular verses.

Don't worry about finding the "perfect" passage—just begin. God often speaks as we seek.

Reflection Questions

1. Why would the Word of God be a delight to you and others (see Week 5)?

2. What options do you have to meditate on what God says?

3. What are some personal verses of courage, patience, humility, etc., you can use to stay grounded in God even through work?

4. If you tend not to think of God regularly throughout the day, what is overshadowing Him?

Week 48
Model Good, Get It Back

Give, and it will be given to you. A good measure, pressed down, shaken together and running over, will be poured into your lap. For with the measure you use, it will be measured to you. —Luke 6:38

"You haven't done anything for me, so why should I do anything for you?"

This question demonstrates a significant psychological principle: We look for reciprocity in relationships and generally mirror back what we're given: For kindness, we give compassion; for cruelty, we deliver harshness.

Jesus understood this element of human nature. In this sense, Luke 6:38 offers some logic around the golden rule that appears earlier in Luke 6:31: "Do to others as you would have them do to you." It's part of what makes His instruction to forgive 77 times—not 7—so mind-blowing (Matthew 18:21-22). If we forgive others to that degree, their subsequent desire to reciprocate in some way potentially translates to an exponential release of emotional burden, dramatically increasing peace and healing.

But Jesus was also getting across the idea that good and evil each have their own reward. Good action and character beget blessings, while evil action and character beget discipline, loss, and suffering. If we want blessings, faith that compels us to reflect God's Spirit through obedience—as best we can in our imperfection—is the only path to get them.

In the business context, Luke 6:38 applies two ways. First, hoarding resources, treating others poorly for our own gain, or looking out only for ourselves ultimately will limit us. If instead we are willing to help, then when we have a need, we will have others to lean on (see Weeks 6, 10 and 17).

Secondly, God sees the giving or effort we put forth on His behalf. Even if others don't respond well and fail to reciprocate, God has a way to correct that injustice and give us the blessing we deserve. No one can thwart His deliverance of that blessing to us. Even if we do not see the advantage in this life through elements like influence or company growth, the blessing waits for us in the next.

Knowing that God's reciprocity is perfect, be encouraged to persist in integrity and do the right thing.

Challenge

There are many ways to do good as an expression of faith. All of them, however, lean on generosity of spirit. Find at least one way to be more generous, such as giving more time, donating a larger amount of money, or offering insight gained through years of experience.

Continue to explore other ways of giving over time. Keep in mind that you can create opportunities as much as you can seek them (see Week 26).

Reflection Questions

1. When was the last time you gave to someone else? Who received your generosity and why?

2. What would you like others on Earth to give you? What would you like from God?

3. What makes it easy (or difficult) for you to give?

4. Are there other ways you could give that you're not using now? If so, what's holding you back from using them?

Week 49
Hold When It Counts, Stay on Mission

Therefore, my dear brothers and sisters, stand firm. Let nothing move you. Always give yourselves fully to the work of the Lord, because you know that your labor in the Lord is not in vain.
—1 Corinthians 15:58

Looking at the first half of 1 Corinthians 15:58, the business world pressures us to change and adapt. And in the negotiation room, refusing to bend at all can cause others to see us as too uncompromising to work with, which can sour a deal.

But if we don't stand firm to an appropriate degree, how else can we prove we are loyal to our values, mission, and goals?

True, there might be times when God grows us and, as a result, our goals, mission, and values all get reoriented. Well-known companies have shown it's possible to incorporate learning and improved sensitivity into rebranding in a way that enhances cultural relevance—PepsiCo's 2021 rebrand of Aunt Jemima to Pearl Milling Company, which aimed to address racial stereotyping, is a prominent example.[57]

But the gains we might get from shifting solely for social approval and sales are never worth a loss of integrity and character. When we're sure we are doing good work (see Week 39), we can commit that work to Him (see Week 50), rather than allowing others to convince us that the only way to succeed is to accept some evil.

Looking at the second half of the verse, no matter what our ventures on this Earth might be, the work of the Lord is most important. That holds when others look down on us or we are weary. It holds, too, even under the temptation of money, fame, power, or anything else that tends to come with corporate wins. Staying laser-focused to come out on top—being saved, and helping others get there, too—applies here more than anywhere else.

Challenge

Any time you must introduce a new idea or do something you know might get pushback at work because it connects to your faith in some way, come up with three rationales for why you want to move forward in your chosen way. This practice helps others understand that you've thought through your decision carefully. It defends your perspective without aggression and strengthens your own faith by clarifying why the action matters to you.

Reflection Questions

1. Have you ever had people tell you that you *had* to compromise? What happened?

2. What are some ways you can be loving to others even as you stand firm?

3. What are some of the advantages of standing firm for God? Disadvantages?

4. Are you currently standing as firm as you want to be for the Lord? Why or why not?

Week 50
Lay It Out Without Division

Commit to the Lord whatever you do, and he will establish your plans. — Proverbs 16:3

Talk of commitment in offices usually ties to getting our individual job done so our team can get a win. It connects to values buy-in, agreement, a willingness to work hard, and trustworthiness: *Can you follow through and not jump ship?*

But additional definitions of "commit" are "pledge" and "devote." By these definitions, if we commit, we're saying that no one else has a claim to us or our resources, or that we are giving ourselves or those resources in totality.

If we humbly commit what we are doing to God, our effort is not divided between Him and someone else. We lay everything out for Him to take.

Yeah, that's a tall demand.

Isn't He worth it?

God doesn't leave our loyalty and service unrewarded. If we offer Him what we have with a devoted spirit, He will bless us.

Consider Cain and Abel (Genesis 4:1-16). Each brother brought a sacrifice to God — Abel gave fat portions from the firstborn of his flock, while Cain offered fruits from his crops. God accepted Abel's sacrifice but rejected Cain's.

Based on Exodus 13:2; 34:19 and Leviticus 2:14, along with the fact the fat from Abel's animals would have been a valuable delicacy, some scholars speculate that Cain's offering might have lacked the quality of Abel's. Cain might not have followed instructions from God exactly as he should have.

But we are told elsewhere in Scripture that Cain didn't bring his crop offering with the same level of faith, and that Cain murdered Abel because "his own actions were evil while his brother's were righteous" (Hebrews 11:4; 1 John 3:11-12).

What each brother sacrificed wasn't the point — *how completely they were committed to God* was.

190

Even though Cain killed Abel in anger, God has always responded well to those who, in full dedication and devotion, hold nothing back from Him. This is why we are reminded in Deuteronomy 4:29 that, if we seek the Lord with all our heart and soul, we'll find Him.

In the context of God's power, Proverbs 16:3 also speaks to the fact that, when we commit ourselves to God, we have access to everything He can do. So, with Him as our partner and *His* will as our priority (see Weeks 30 and 34), there is no way to fail.

You might not be sure yet how to commit your full plan or project to God. You might not have known Him long enough, or perhaps you are going through a period where you have doubts that God will be with you (see Weeks 12 and 21).

But the beauty of Proverbs 16:3 is that it's a standing promise. God has no intent of revoking it, and He understands exactly where you are at. Just start where you are. He'll reveal Himself, soften your heart, and take residence there in His time.

Challenge

Before beginning a task or activity, ask whether you can genuinely commit it to God. If anything—ego, fear, or outside pressure—is holding you back, name it and take steps to come into better alignment with Him.

Reflection Questions

1. How can you show God and others that you have committed what you do to Him?

2. What work have you resisted committing to God? Why?

3. What stories from Scripture show servants of God behaving in full commitment?

4. If people do not commit their work to God, what else might they commit it to?

Week 51
Watch God, Copy Him, Stay the Course

Follow God's example, therefore, as dearly beloved children and walk in the way of love, just as Christ loved us and gave himself up for us as a fragrant offering and sacrifice to God.
—Ephesians 5:1-2

Children watch and copy *everything*. Robin Williams got laughs about it in his 1986 stand-up comedy skit on fatherhood—he recounted how his young son repeated the expletive Williams let fly after someone cut him off in traffic.[58]

Ephesians 5:1-2 reminds us that we're children of God who ought to watch and copy Him. Doing so ensures that He has good representatives on Earth who reflect Who He is.

But professionals often seek to imitate not God, but leaders who seem to have found success (see Week 20). They pore over the leaders' routines and processes in the hope that they'll win out like the leaders did. It's arguably easier to find someone imitating Elon Musk or Jeff Bezos than it is to find someone who wholeheartedly imitates God.

In this reality, we shouldn't be surprised if people don't understand why we're following God's rules (see Week 5). We likewise shouldn't be surprised if we have to stand like Elijah, a sole prophet of God surrounded by the 450 prophets of Baal.

But remember what happened to those 450 men.

In the end, God used Elijah to defeat them all.

Stay the course. Commit (see Week 50). If we set the example, we'll have victory over the 450 men, and somewhere in the office, there might be a single person who, as Elisha before Elijah, is watching, needs us, and can take up our torch when it matters.

Challenge

Identify three traits you believe best reflect God's character and three ways you see Him consistently working (His "patterns of behavior"). Use these as spiritual guardrails throughout your day (see Week 5). If you notice your actions straying from Who God is or how He moves, take it as a prompt to realign.

Reflection Questions

1. Which people have you been tempted to imitate? Why?

2. What types of things can you do to imitate Jesus?

3. What keeps you from acting more like Jesus?

4. How might you strike a balance between imitating and prioritizing God and finding valuable mentorship with others (see Week 20)?

Week 52
Say What God Gives You

When you are brought before synagogues, rulers and authorities, do not worry about how you will defend yourselves or what you will say, for the Holy Spirit will teach you at that time what you should say. — Luke 12:11-12

Some people are natural speakers. They can get up at a conference or in a meeting and own the room as easily as if they were eating a popsicle.

If that's you, awesome. If it's not you, welcome to the Nervous Norm and Nancy Club, where every time a person has to speak, they overthink everything, constantly rehearse, and generally feel like vomiting all over their shoes.

Moses knew something about feeling like a poor speaker. He even pointed out to God he was a crappy communicator, hoping He'd send someone else to confront Pharaoh.

But God wouldn't take excuses. He sent Moses to Egypt to get the Israelites anyway (see Week 29).

Yet, God didn't send Moses because He wanted Moses to sweat bullets. God sent Moses because He was fully prepared to help Moses communicate well. He knew His power could overcome whatever faults or shortcomings Moses had.

What makes us so different from Moses?

Not much.

That's why Jesus reassures the disciples as He does, not only in Luke 12:11-12, but also again in Mark 13:11 with even greater clarity about the persecution He knew they would encounter: "Whenever you are arrested and brought to trial, do not worry beforehand about what to say. Just say whatever is given you at the time, for it is not you speaking, but the Holy Spirit."

Whether you're presenting quarterly results, defending your values in a tough meeting, or calling out something unjust, Jesus understands we have the same assignment of convincing authorities. He gets that the same fears will try to choke us. But the Holy Spirit that was with the twelve will speak through us, too, so long as we are willing to open our mouths. This includes in the office, where our work can be a means to accomplish His larger goals.

Even if you don't have to stand up in Egypt, stand up.

Challenge

The next time you must speak, try intentionally stopping your practice or review just before you feel fully ready. This isn't about being careless or putting yourself or your work at risk. It's about creating a little space to lean more on God than you're used to.

Remember that overly polished presentations can sometimes feel less relatable. Focus on letting God guide you, and prioritize the sincerity, passion, and accuracy He helps you cultivate over perfection.

Reflection Questions

1. What authorities or leaders do you routinely come in front of or present for?

2. How do you typically prepare to speak or present before these authorities?

3. Have you ever gone in front of your authorities without worry? If so, what helped you stay calm? If not, what caused your worry (see Week 30)?

4. Besides Moses, who else in the Bible did God help to speak or serve with courage?

About Faithful on the Clock

Faithful on the Clock is a Christian podcast meant to get your faith and work aligned. You won't find any mantras or hacks in the show—just Scripture-based insights to help you grow yourself, your company, and your relationship with God. If you want out of the worldly hamster wheel and want to work with purpose, Faithful on the Clock is the show for you. Hosted by freelance business writer Wanda Marie Thibodeaux.

Join Faithful on the Clock online!

Main podcast site: faithfulontheclock.captivate.fm
Sister site: faithfulontheclock.com
Substack: faithfulontheclock.substack.com

Social Media:
Threads - @faithfulontheclock
Instagram - @faithfulontheclock
Pinterest - @faithfulontheclock
Facebook - @faithfulontheclock
LinkedIn Groups – Faithful on the Clock
(linkedin.com/groups/12553140)

About the Author

Wanda Marie Thibodeaux is a freelance writer helping Christian organizations and professionals communicate with clarity and purpose—while also offering original devotional videos, essays, and reflections to support those carrying unseen emotional weight in their leadership journey. Helping people reclaim joy is her calling.

Since 2006, Thibodeaux has worked with a full range of clients to create website landing pages, product descriptions, articles, ebooks, and other content. She also served as a daily columnist for Inc.com for three years, where she specialized in content on business leadership, psychology, neuroscience, and behavior. Her bylined work or ghostwriting has appeared in publications such as *Forbes*, *Entrepreneur*, and *Harvard Business Review*.

Join Thibodeaux online!

Business site: takingdictation.com
Author site: wandathibodeaux.com

Social Media:
Threads - @takingdictation
Instagram - @takingdictation
Pinterest - @takingdictation
Facebook - @WandaMThibodeaux
LinkedIn - @WandaThibodeaux

Additional Resources

B The Change

Christian Blue

Christian Business Men's Connection

Christian Executives Organization

Christian Women Business Organization

Christian Leadership Alliance

Christian Professional and Academic Societies

C-Suite for Christ

Faith Driven Entrepreneur

MinistryWatch: 30 Largest Christian Advocacy Organizations

The Christian Business Network

Endnotes

[1] Boyton, E. (2022, April 18). *Taking Breaks Is Good for Your Brain—Here's Why*. Right as Rain. rightasrain.uwmedicine.org/mind/well-being/taking-breaks.

[2] [Pathway Church PTBO]. (2023, September 4). *Start Fresh—Tim Doremus*. [Video]. YouTube. youtube.com/watch?v=T-1KrPhCz9k.

[3] [The Chosen]. (2023, March 19). *Why Haven't You Healed Me? (The Chosen Scene)*. [Video]. YouTube. youtube.com/watch?v=KZDvcEkjthA&t=34s.

[4] Thibodeaux, W. (2025, January 2). *This is the first car I ever owned*. [URL attached] [Post]. Instagram. instagram.com/p/DEUooiVxSTd/?utm_source=ig_web_copy_link.

[5] Thibodeaux, W. (2024, August 2). *You Don't Need to Be More Grateful. You Need to Learn What Has More Value*. Faithful on the Clock. faithfulontheclock.com/freecontent/you-dont-need-to-be-more-grateful-you-need-to-learn-what-has-more-value.

[6] Thibodeaux, W. (2023, September). *I love this so much. A big part of the Christian church centers on reactionary service. Find the homeless, find*. [URL attached] [Post]. LinkedIn. linkedin.com/posts/wandathibodeaux_megachurch-will-open-auto-repair-shop-to-activity-7057776078978748417-kQyr/?utm_source=share&utm_medium=member_desktop.

[7] Usable Knowledge. (2017, November 20). *A Better Way of Thinking*. Harvard Graduate School of Education. gse.harvard.edu/ideas/usable-knowledge/17/11/better-way-thinking.

[8] Thibodeaux, W. [Faithful on the Clock]. (2025, August 26). *How to Avoid Cat-Poster Christianity*. [Podcast]. faithfulontheclock.captivate.fm/episode/how-to-avoid-cat-poster-christianity.

[9] Thibodeaux, W. [Faithful on the Clock]. (2025, March 10). *Escaping George Bailey Syndrome to Save Your God-Given Dream*. [Podcast]. faithfulontheclock.captivate.fm/episode/escaping-george-bailey-syndrome-to-save-your-god-given-dream.

[10] Thibodeaux, W. (2025, March 10). *Ever think more than one good thing matters at once?* [URL attached] [Post]. Instagram. instagram.com/reel/DHBdf5-iAf5/?utm_source=ig_web_copy_link&igsh=MzRlODBiNWFlZA==.

[11] Wakeling, K. (2019, May 28). *Pythagoras & the Music of the Spheres.* Aurora Orchestra. auroraorchestra.com/2019/05/pythagoras-the-music-of-the-spheres.

[12] Frongia, F., Forti, L., and Arru, L. (2020, October 13). *Plant Signaling & Behavior.* National Library of Medicine. ncbi.nlm.nih.gov/pmc/articles/PMC7671032/#:~:text=Plants%20emit%20also%20ultrasonic%20vibrations,the%20stem%20of%20the%20plant.&text=Plants%20release%20sound%20emissions%20from,in%20response%20to%20different%20situations.

[13] Varga, T. (n.d.). *The Ringing Rocks of the USA Sound Like a Bell When Struck.* Earthly Mission. earthlymission.com/ringing-rocks-usa-sound-bell-struck-hit-hammer-geology.

[14] Graber, M. (n.d.). *The Evolution of the ISO Principle in Music Therapy and Music Listening.* Central Ohio Music Therapy. centralohiomusictherapy.com/the-evolution-of-the-iso-principle-in-music-therapy-and-music-listening.

[15] Wolf, J. (2023, February 16). *Is kindness contagious?* UCLA Magazine. universityofcalifornia.edu/news/kindness-contagious.

[16] Neuroscientifically Challenged. (n.d.). *Know Your Brain: Reward System.* neuroscientificallychallenged.com/posts/know-your-brain-reward-system.

[17] Zhang, M., Zhang, Y., and Kong, Y. (2020, May 18). *Interaction between social pain and physical pain.* Tsinghua University Press. journals.sagepub.com/doi/full/10.26599/BSA.2019.9050023.

[18] Thibodeaux, W. (2022, August 11). *3 Massive Reasons It's Tough to Be Kind at Work.* [Newsletter]. LinkedIn. linkedin.com/pulse/3-massive-reasons-its-tough-kind-work-wanda-thibodeaux/?trackingId=ADAYTi9bRSq4ek6oBbKLSA%3D%3D.

[19] Thibodeaux, W. (2025, March 19). *What God Gives You to Fight With.* [URL attached] [Post]. Instagram.

instagram.com/reel/DHYORNhNlMV/?utm_source=ig_web_copy_link&igsh=MzRlODBiNWFlZA==.

20 Wilson, M. (2024, August 27). *Treasures in Clay Jars.* Biblical Archaeology Society. biblicalarchaeology.org/daily/biblical-artifacts/artifacts-and-the-bible/treasures-in-clay-jars.

21 Torrice, M. (2009, October 5). *Buried Treasure Fills in Ancient Roman Puzzle.* Science. science.org/content/article/buried-treasure-fills-ancient-roman-puzzle.

22 Pruitt, S. (2019, February 20). *What Did Jesus Look Like?* History.com. https://www.history.com/articles/what-did-jesus-look-like.

23 Thibodeaux, W. [Faithful on the Clock]. (2025, July 28). *Leadership, Meaning, and Making Space for Questions.* [Podcast]. faithfulontheclock.captivate.fm/episode/leadership-meaning-and-making-space-for-questions.

24 Thibodeaux, W. (2024, October 24). *Ambition Isn't Always Good. Here's How to Keep It Positive.* [Newsletter]. LinkedIn. linkedin.com/pulse/ambition-isnt-always-good-heres-how-keep-positive-wanda-thibodeaux-hblgc/?trackingId=PP9KHBYFQpKDVpuIVvHdBA%3D%3D.

25 [Woodcrest Church]. (2025, September 7). *Woodcrest Church 9-7-2025.* [YouTube]. youtube.com/watch?v=fxFUCDVBJuc.

26 Graham, B. (1996, January 12). *What Was So Bad About Biblical Tax Collectors?* Greensboro. greensboro.com/what-was-so-bad-about-biblical-tax-collectors/article_9adbf182-ba65-5b32-a964-3b1e6438ccb3.html.

27 Byerly, J. (2017, November 4). *The Janitor Who Helped Put a Man on the Moon.* From the Green Notebook. fromthegreennotebook.com/2017/11/04/the-janitor-who-help-put-a-man-on-the-moon.

28 Van Tilburg, W., Igou, E., and Panjwani, M. (2022, March 8). *Boring People: Stereotype Characteristics, Interpersonal Attributions, and Social Reactions.* Personality and Social Psychology Bulletin, 49(9). journals.sagepub.com/doi/10.1177/01461672221079104.

29 Thibodeaux, W. [Faithful on the Clock]. (2025, July 28). *Leadership, Meaning, and Making Space for Questions.* [Podcast].

faithfulontheclock.captivate.fm/episode/leadership-meaning-and-making-space-for-questions.

30 Ziegler, B. (2023, May 25). *When Twitter's Watching, Companies Behave Better.* The Wall Street Journal. wsj.com/articles/twitter-social-media-company-behavior-a1163e28.

31 Croston, G. (2012, November 29). *The Thing We Fear More Than Death.* Psychology Today. psychologytoday.com/us/blog/the-real-story-risk/201211/the-thing-we-fear-more-death.

32 Buhler, P. and Worden, J. (2016, February 18). *The Cost of Poor Communication.* Society for Human Resource Management. shrm.org/topics-tools/news/organizational-employee-development/cost-poor-communication.

33 Thibodeaux, W. (2024, November 13). *Do you believe God will provide for you?* [URL attached] [Post]. Instagram. instagram.com/reel/DCT47j8iIAN/?utm_source=ig_web_copy_link.

34 Thibodeaux, W. [Faithful on the Clock]. (2021, October 18). *An Ever-Present Help.* [Podcast]. faithfulontheclock.captivate.fm/episode/an-ever-present-help.

35 Thibodeaux, W. (2023, March 8). *Jesus Conquered a Tree.* [URL attached] [Post]. Instagram. instagram.com/p/Cphhw2Ett2e.

36 Thibodeaux, W. (2025, July 26). *Have You Blessed God Back Today?* Faithful on the Clock. faithfulontheclock.com/freecontent/have-you-blessed-god-back-today.

37 Thibodeaux, W. [Faithful on the Clock]. (2025, September 8). *Bleeding Need: The Woman with the Hemorrhage.* [Podcast]. faithfulontheclock.captivate.fm/episode/bleeding-need-the-woman-with-the-hemorrhage.

38 [Popcorn Picks]. (2025, July 24). *Patch Faces the Medical Board (Incredible Acting) | Patch Adams.* [Video]. YouTube. youtube.com/watch?v=eZbsfzdjZ2Q.

39 Adams, P. (2025). *Patch Adams.* The Gesundheit! Institute. https://www.patchadams.org/patch-adams.

40 Martino, J., Pegg, J., and Frates, E. (2015, October 7). *The Connection Prescription: Using the Power of Social Interactions and the Deep Desire for*

Connectedness to Empower Health and Wellness. National Institutes of Health. pmc.ncbi.nlm.nih.gov/articles/PMC6125010.

[41] Krug, E. (2023, November 15). *It's time to harness the power of connection for our health and wellbeing.* World Health Organization. who.int/news-room/commentaries/detail/it-s-time-to-harness-the-power-of-connection-for-our-health-and-well-being.

[42] Centers for Disease Control and Prevention. (2024, May 15). *Social Connection.* cdc.gov/social-connectedness/about/index.html.

[43] Thibodeaux, W. [Faithful on the Clock]. (2024, September 9). *Debunking the Prosperity Gospel.* [Podcast]. faithfulontheclock.captivate.fm/episode/debunking-the-prosperity-gospel.

[44] Thibodeaux, W. [Faithful on the Clock]. (2022, December 7). *Not Your Vending Machine.* [Video]. YouTube. youtube.com/watch?v=mD2qjSXq82k.

[45] McCurry, J. (2017, October 5). *Japanese woman 'dies from overwork' after logging 159 hours of overtime in a month.* The Guardian. theguardian.com/world/2017/oct/05/japanese-woman-dies-overwork-159-hours-overtime.

[46] Pega, F., et al. (2021, September). *Global, regional, and national burdens of ischemic heart disease and stroke attributable to exposure to long work hours for 194 countries, 2000-2016: A systemic analysis from WHO/ILO Joint Estimates of the Work-related Burden of Disease and Injury.* Environ Int. pmc.ncbi.nlm.nih.gov/articles/PMC8204267.

[47] World Health Organization. (2021, May 17). *Long working hours increasing deaths from heart disease and stroke: WHO, ILO.* who.int/news/item/17-05-2021-long-working-hours-increasing-deaths-from-heart-disease-and-stroke-who-ilo#:~:text=Long%20working%20hours%20led%20to,the%20largest%20occupational%20disease%20burden.

[48] Brown, L. (2020, December 4). *The Power of Rest.* Creative Plus Business. creativeplusbusiness.com/the-power-of-rest.

[49] Thibodeaux, W. [Faithful on the Clock]. (2024, January 10). *An Idea Worth Saving.* [Video]. YouTube. youtube.com/watch?v=c3AhoKNrsdg.

50 Thibodeaux, W. (2022, November 14). *God Would Throw a Party for You.* [URL attached] [Post]. Instagram. instagram.com/p/Ck8TtfmgbGN/?utm_source=ig_web_copy_link&igsh =MzRlODBiNWFlZA==.

51 Thibodeaux, W. (2022, December 28). *Make Sure He's Invited.* [URL attached] [Post]. Instagram. instagram.com/reel/CmukcNgjzZo/?utm_source=ig_web_copy_link.

52 Thibodeaux, W. (2023, April 19). *Relatable.* [URL attached] [Post]. Instagram. instagram.com/reel/CrNrWBNM2Iw/?utm_source=ig_web_copy_link.

53 Thibodeaux. W. (2025, August 6). *He'll Take It.* Substack. open.substack.com/pub/faithfulontheclock/p/hell-take-it?r=ga7sq&utm_campaign=post&utm_medium=web&showWelcomeO nShare=true.

54 Thibodeaux, W. (2023, May 17). *Walk Around the City.* [URL attached] [Post]. Instagram. instagram.com/reel/CsVjjVNt1W6/?utm_source=ig_web_copy_link&igs h=MzRlODBiNWFlZA==.

55 Thibodeaux, W. (2023, August 3). *Inversion Thinking: What It Is and How It Can Create Superior Decision Outcomes.* [Newsletter]. LinkedIn. linkedin.com/pulse/inversion-thinking-what-how-can-create-superior-wanda-thibodeaux/?trackingId=wJpAAeHrT3WmISREbD1THg%3D%3D.

56 Grady, C. (2017, September 13). *The convoluted world of best-seller lists, explained.* Vox. vox.com/culture/2017/9/13/16257084/bestseller-lists-explained.

57 Diaz, J. (2021, February 10). *Aunt Jemima No More; Pancake Brand Renamed Pearl Milling Company.* National Public Radio. npr.org/2021/02/10/966166648/aunt-jemima-no-more-pancake-brand-renamed-pearl-milling-company.

58 [A Dram a Day]. (2016, October 16). *Robin Williams on fatherhood.* [Video]. YouTube. youtube.com/watch?v=ykq8IkiCgFw.

www.ingramcontent.com/pod-product-compliance
Lightning Source LLC
Chambersburg PA
CBHW080129150626
46550CB00018B/2923